TRADITIONAL DANISH SWEATERS

First published in the United States of America in 2019 by
Trafalgar Square Books
North Pomfret, Vermont 05053

Originally published in Danish as *Strik danske stjernetrøjer.*

Copyright © 2017 Vivian Høxbro and Turbineforlaget
English translation © 2019 Trafalgar Square Books

ISBN: 978-1-57076-924-5

Library of Congress Control Number: 2019937905

Text and designs: © Vivian Høxbro
Illustrations: © Vivian Høxbro
Charts: Design-Partner, www.design-partner.dk
Photography: © Ingrid Riis, www.ingridfotografi.dk; except for page 11: © Lars Dalby
Nielsen, www.larsdalby.dk, and pages 13-77: © Vivian Høxbro
Danish editor: Merete Kjær Petersen
Interior graphic design: Anja Søe Jensen
Translation into English: Carol Huebscher Rhoades

Printed in Hong Kong

10 9 8 7 6 5 4 3 2

PUBLISHED WITH THE SUPPORT OF

Queen Margrethe and Prince Henrik's Foundation

Farumgaard Foundation

Aage and Johanne Louis-Hansen's Foundation

This work was supported with funds from Copydan distributed by the Author

Fund of the Danish Authors' Association

The State Arts Foundation, in the form of a work grant

VIVIAN HØXBRO

Vivian Høxbro has worked as a knitting designer for more than 30 years, both for yarn companies and freelance. She has written 10 knitting books, published by Norwegian, American, Japanese, and Danish companies. In 2000, she presented her own kit collection, which continues to be sold. During the same time period, she has also taught and made presentations in Scandinavia as well as in the USA and Japan.

www.viv.dk

CONTENTS

Knitting Books

At the front, you can see the Knitting Book for School and Household *by Sine Andresen, published in 1846. Behind that is the* Instructor's Book for Female Handcrafts *from 1875, which was bound together with the* Illustrated Knitting Book, *from 1883.*

FOREWORD

A number of years ago, I visited Falster Minder Museum in Nykøbing, Denmark for the Sunday Weekly magazine. Birgit Schytt, the textile curator, opened drawer after drawer containing knitted sweaters (called "night sweaters") from nineteenth-century women's traditional wardrobes, which she clearly venerated. All the sweaters were single-color—many green, some red, and a few blue or black. Most were knitted with only knit and purl stitches, while others featured traveling stitches. They were quite felted and torn, but they all shared a fantastic wealth of patterns.

I felt that messages to me flew out of the drawers, both from the sweaters and from the people who had knitted them, and I was deeply moved. Think of the women who, almost 200 years ago, had designed these unbelievable patterns! The knitters of the sweaters came alive for me. I sensed that some had knitted out of duty, some for love of handwork. On some of the sweaters, the patterns were beautifully formed; others were less skillfully worked. Some of the patterns were perfectly designed, others asymmetrical and imprecise in their construction. What more could these sweaters tell us?

I later had the opportunity to visit the Lolland-Falster Museum every Thursday for more than a year. After that, I visited several other museums in Denmark—on Zealand (Hillerød and Kalundborg), Fyn (Odense), and Jutland (Ribe, Varde, Herning and Holstebro). I studied sweater after sweater. I photographed, sketched, and knitted all the motifs. This led to the documentation of 87 complete knitted night sweaters, as well as a number of sleeves and front pieces (*brystduge*). In the course of my research, I was greatly privileged to be able to examine at least half of the preserved Danish night sweaters. Most of the preserved sweaters are stored on Falster (where I live) and Lolland, and they are the backbone of this book.

These sweaters, which our great- and great-great great grandmothers wore, can, with a few small adjustments, be worn with style today. This book includes patterns for some of the old sweaters in contemporary sizing. Stars were a fashionable motif in nineteenth-century knitting, and star designs embellish the new sweaters in this book. You'll also find a multitude of star motifs to choose from. I hope the traditional patterns will inspire you to try new designs!

Traditional night sweaters are so beautiful and the techniques so sophisticated—they deserve notice, and this book is intended to pay tribute to them. It's important to remember that our past is what makes us who we are; and for those of us who love knitting, it enriches our work every time we learn something new about knitting history.

Best wishes,

Vivian Høxbro

NIGHT SWEATER PORTRAITS

In this section of the book, you'll find portraits of some of the many original night sweaters which can be found preserved in our Danish museums. Most of them are carefully stored away and not available to everyone, but here you can see them together with a short summary of their characteristics.

C = Circumference
TL = Total length
SL = Sleeve length (from top of sleeve to bottom of cuff)

At each museum, the sweaters have been catalogued with unique numbers. These museum numbers are listed alongside the picture of each sweater, and referenced throughout the book.

As might be expected, the old sweaters were photographed under all kinds of light conditions. However, I think these small "portraits" will give an idea of how much these sweaters varied, even though they also have many similarities to each other. I especially want to show how lovely they are and how cleverly they were made.

PREFACE BY MAJ RINGGAARD

Throughout my many years studying historical knitting, particularly 17th-century silk knitted shirts and the corresponding wool night sweaters, I've been deeply fascinated by both the many beautiful variations on one theme and especially the fine handwork. The small details—even if a pair of sweaters looks the same at first glance—reveal individual methods of solving technical knitting challenges in the task at hand. Small differences in shaping, pattern, and edgings, how increases were spaced, how motifs were placed, etc., distinguish each sweater from the rest. Details such as "false seams," or narrow panels placed where a seam would normally be sewn, were not only decorative but made it much easier to see where and when increases and decreases should be made.

These sweaters were not colorful, with large variegated patterns. Quite the opposite: a defining characteristic is the choice of a single color, allowing subtle effects to play out across stockinette and reverse stockinette sections, or simple relief patterns of traveling stitches. Originally worked in stockinette with smooth silk yarns or long-fibered wool, their rich luster shimmered and showed off these pattern effects. In certain newer sweaters, people used a crimpier wool, so this effect was not as obvious, but that didn't hold knitters back from knitting the traditional patterns. All these sweaters had their own personal touches. At the same time, they showcase the skill of the knitters who explored the possibilities of the techniques and found innovative solutions which were lost in more recent times. They clearly challenged themselves to address difficulties in new ways, creating sweaters with almost no sewing as they tested intricate patterns.

I have often been taken by how inspiring they are and have thought that someone ought to make the diverse, beautiful details of these sweaters appealing for modern knitters. So it was such a pleasure to meet Vivian, who was at least as taken with these sweaters as I was, even though they weren't as colorful as Vivian's own designs. It was inspiring to accompany Vivian, with her great enthusiasm, to research the sweaters across museum collections and to observe her sense for the small details as she meticulously worked to discern the patterns on heavily felted sweaters. We discussed whether one could observe any special distinctions, if there were extra clever knitters in certain regions—or perhaps some museum collections had many particularly fine sweaters only owing to the fact that someone had had the sense to acquire these sweaters quickly, before they disappeared into the shoddy mills or the materials were reused during wartime.

This book contains not only knitting patterns, but easily understood instructions for contemporary knitters covering well over a hundred relief and damask designs, all of which Vivian has observed on the many sweaters she has analyzed in Danish museums. In addition, there are many sketches and photos, so you'll really get a feeling for the immense diversity of the sweaters' patterning. With this book, these fine night sweaters are now easily available to anyone who wishes to knit them with modern yarn in contemporary sizes. It's a worthwhile read both for those who only want to learn a bit of history, and for those who want to construct their own night sweaters.

Look through, enjoy, and let yourself be inspired by this book. The original Danish title of this book, *Star Sweaters*, was chosen because most of the garments have star patterns; the old words *nattrøie* or *bindtrøie* ("night sweater" or "knitted sweater") are no longer commonly used in Danish; and, of course, they are star-quality sweaters.

Maj Ringgaard
Ph.D. Textile Conservator
The National Museum of Denmark

HILLERØD SWEATER

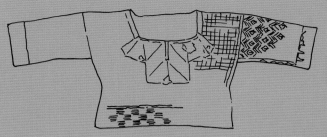

Origin: Unknown.
Museum number: 93-1924.
Conserved in: Museum Nordsjælland (North Zealand).

Measurements: C: 30 in / 76 cm; TL: 12 in / 30.5 cm; SL: 7¾ in / 19.5 cm.
Color: Red.
Knitting gauge: 36 sts = 4 in / 10 cm.
Pattern: Vertical panels and edge patterns on the body.
Main pattern and vertical panels on the sleeves.

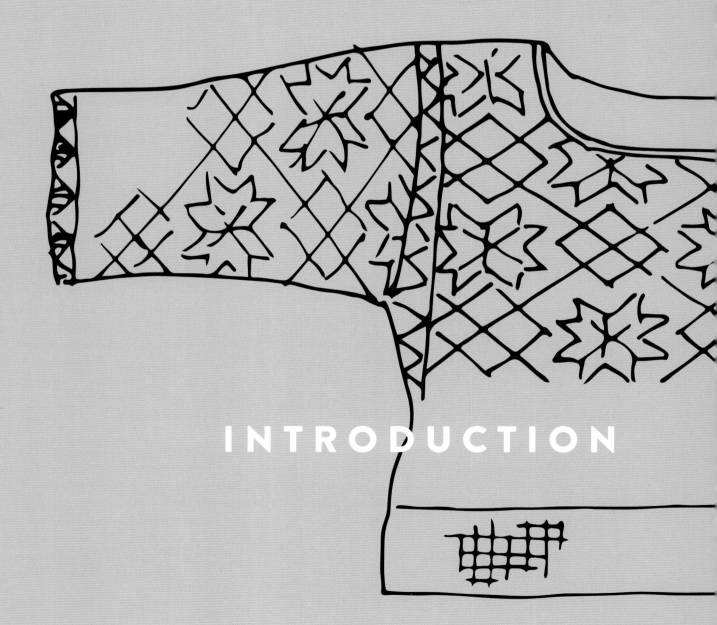

INTRODUCTION

200 PATTERNS FROM HISTORIC SWEATERS

200-YEAR-OLD WOMEN'S SWEATERS

The sweaters in this book are from the 19th century: "night sweaters," as they were once called, which have roots deep in Danish history. Yes, they are single-color—minimalist, you might say, with quite artfully designed relief patterns. You could also find them in south Sweden (where these garments are referred to as *spedetröjor*) and in Norway—both areas that were considered Danish territory at one time or another, where women knitted sweaters as part of traditional folk dress. Similar sweaters were worn by men, at least up to the beginning of the 19th century, but I have concentrated only on women's sweaters.

Single-color women's sweaters like these, whether Danish, Norwegian, or Swedish, went out of fashion at the end of the 19th century. They were discarded, deconstructed so the materials could be reused, or, in the best case, forgotten but conserved in our museums.

Beautiful, multicolored patterned sweaters from the Shetland Islands, the Faroes, Norway, Sweden, and Finland are easily recognizable. Most of them were originally men's sweaters, and were often lavishly embellished with motifs. In Denmark, we've found one sweater with multicolored knitting, specifically from Sejerø, dating from 1908—and it was a man's sweater, too.

KNITTED SWEATERS IN OTHER SCANDINAVIAN COUNTRIES

Sweaters from the Shetland Islands use colors in a very distinctive way, inspired by the location and landscapes. In Norway, the traditional knitted sweater (*koften*) has survived, and, originally part of men's traditional folk costumes, it has become a common everyday sweater for both men and women. It is, quite simply, a living part of contemporary international style, as well as a signifier of Norwegian national identity—just think of the lice sweater (*lusekofta*).

What connects these sweater styles is that traditional pattern motifs were used and reused, redesigned and

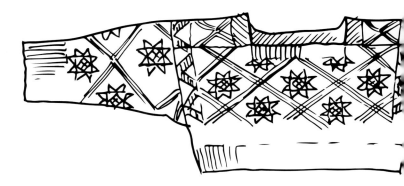

referenced and given new life. Now they're recognized all over the knitting world, while Danish traditional sweaters have been consigned to oblivion—not least because Danish people simply stopped wearing them. I hope to remedy that situation with this book!

PATTERN TREASURES AT MUSEUMS

When night sweaters disappeared from the Danish sartorial landscape, their patterns did also. I had no luck finding written or sketched patterns for them from the time period when they were knitted and worn. However, more than 150 sweaters and some knitted sleeves have been preserved in Danish museums. In Mariann Ploug's book, *Knitted Night Sweaters in Danish Museums* (1979), approximately 136 items are listed. The same book lists 37 sweaters from museums on Lolland and Falster, but by the time I visited them, these museums had a total of 60 complete sweaters. That means 23 new items have been acquired since 1979, and with any luck the situation is the same in other museums around the country.

The sweaters, now museum items, are fragile, and not many museums put them on display. They typically end up packed in acid-free paper in cardboard boxes, tucked away in storage areas. If you have the opportunity, you can see how they were knitted—how fine and light the yarn was, how thin the needles must have been, and how complex the designs can get. The patterns have common features as well as local influences, but the clearest shared feature is the rich designs. Danish knitters should be proud of this heritage, which deserves our admiration.

They are, nevertheless, not available for everyone to see, which is one of the reasons I wrote this book. Contemporary knitters deserve to have the fine art of our foremothers' knitting recognized and available to be appreciated—this book offers a glimpse into our own past.

200 PATTERNS

I have collected 200 patterns that were used for Danish night sweaters, primarily from Falster and Lolland. They are shown on pages 78-139 as knitted samples with corresponding charts, grouped according to where they appeared—as edges, horizontal and vertical panels, background patterns, or as decorative stars.

KNITTING INSTRUCTIONS

In this book, you'll also find five traditional sweater patterns reconstructed with contemporary sizing, plus four new sweaters as well as one top and one stole designed with traditional design principles in mind—complete pattern instructions are included for all of them.

Specific knitting techniques used for the original sweaters are explained on pages 60-77. Additional knitting help, abbreviations, and a chart symbol key are provided at the end of the book.

This book is primarily a pattern and knitting book. I am not a historian; I've worked all my life as a designer and pattern writer for hand knitters. However, I've included a little knitting history, found in various sources I discovered as I worked on this book.

Read the sections in any order you like. Use the motifs for your own designs. And knit traditional Danish sweaters of your own!

LEESTRUP SWEATER

Origin: Leestrup, Zealand.
Private ownership.

Measurements: C: 33 in / 84 cm; TL: 14¼ in / 36 cm; SL: 8 in / 20.5 cm.
Color: Red with silk ribbons.
Knitting gauge: 36 sts and 60 rows = 4 x 4 in / 10 x 10 cm.
Patterns: Edge patterns and vertical panels on the body. The shoulder pieces are knitted together with the shoulders stitches from back and front. Traveling stitch and star motifs on the sleeves.

Danish
NIGHT SWEATERS

A NIGHT SWEATER?

> **Nattrøie**, an old term for a (short) garment (sweater with sleeves), worn at night (over an undergarment) and sometimes worn during the day (under the ordinary outer garments). (From the Dictionary of Danish Language)

KNITTED BLOUSES

When I think of the term "night sweater," I visualize a knitted blouse. By the end of the 16th century, wealthy people wore sweaters knitted in fine silk or worsted-spun yarn. This style endured until the end of the 18th century, when similar sweaters knitted with wool yarn were worn by those less-well-off in society.

WHY ARE THEY CALLED NIGHT SWEATERS?

Beloved children have many names, according to an old Scandinavian saying. These old sweaters also have many names. If you look at them in museum catalogues, you'll find them listed as, for example, knitted sweaters, with several versions of the word "knitted" (*striktrøjer, strixtrøjer, bindtrøjer, lænketrøjer, pindtrøjer*, and, of course, *nattrøjer*—night sweaters).

Perhaps the name "night sweaters" was used to distinguish between these sweaters and expensive imported sweaters, which were not likely to have been worn at night—on the contrary, they were bought to be shown off and were probably the most expensive items of clothing a woman owned. Ordinary night sweaters were very much inspired by the silk sweaters of the upper class. It was only natural that they also became known as night sweaters.

BOTH A DAY AND A NIGHT SWEATER

When I talk about night sweaters, it's clear to me that at first people often believe I mean Scandinavian bed jackets—those pink fluffy garments in the style our great-grandmothers wore when there was frost on the windows. But no, night sweaters were not bed jackets.

The Danish word *nattrøje* literally translates as "night jacket" or "night shirt." In the early history of these knitted garments, the style was more akin to a shirt or tunic. The fabric, often knitted with silk, was very fine in both quality and density. Later, the same name was used for the more close-fitting short jackets knitted with wool which we have termed "night sweaters" in this book.

Despite being called night sweaters, these garments were also worn during the day. For farmers in the 1800s, there simply was no difference between night and day garments—at least not until the end of the century, when true night garments gradually came into fashion.

Ideas about sleeping with or without clothing have changed over time. In the past, especially during long, dark Danish winters, people took off only as many garments at night as deemed necessary. When it was cold, night sweaters warmed the upper part of the body. For the most part, people slept sitting up in alcoves, so warm clothes

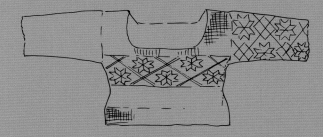

Origin: Nakskov, Lolland.
Museum number: LFS 8868.
Conserved in: Museum Lolland-Falster.

Measurements: C: 30 in / 76 cm; TL: 13¾ in / 35 cm; SL: 8¼ in / 21 cm.
Color: Green.
Knitting gauge: 28 sts and 48 rows = 4 x 4 in / 10 x 10 cm.
Patterns: Traveling stitch and star motifs; edge patterns on the body. Traveling stitch and star motifs on the sleeves.

were beneficial. Why did they sit up? Many suffered from various illnesses such as tuberculous, bronchitis, and/or other lung problems as a consequence of drafts, cold, and hard work. In order to breathe in enough air while asleep, and to make it easier to cough, people sat up.

PART OF THE COSTUME

During the day, people in most parts of Denmark wore night sweaters as part of the rest of their outfit. Women's traditional dress consisted of an inner shift or a bodice. The night sweater was worn over that, and then, over it, came a long skirt with an apron. A tight-fitting vest could be worn over the night sweater; a scarf surrounded the neck, and the head was usually covered by a cap and cap linen. Naturally, there were big differences between the various provinces around the country, depending on the economy and the style of each place. But all over Denmark, you could find the most unbelievably fine patterned sweaters and distinctive stylings.

You might wonder why women devoted so much imagination and energy to knitting all these elegant patterns, when the rest of the outfit only allowed the sleeves or part of them to be seen. My guess is that, then as now, people simply had the need to create something beautiful—a desire for aesthetic appeal. If we have to use our energy for producing food and clothing, we also want beauty.

WHAT A NIGHT SWEATER LOOKS LIKE

DAMASK PATTERNS

I have described what night sweaters worn by peasants looked like, but naturally there are many exceptions to the general rule. Knitted night sweaters worn by most people were single-color and usually decorated with ingenious patterns. They were knitted with white wool yarn and then dyed. A characteristic common to all of them was that they were knitted with patterns using knit and purl stitches, or damask knitting, which, as the name implies, was inspired by damask weaving. That weaving technique, similar to knit-and-purl knitted designs, is characterized by its relief work. However, some sweaters had only a few patterns.

Undyed sleeve from South Falster, probably from the end of the 1700s (FMN 1108).

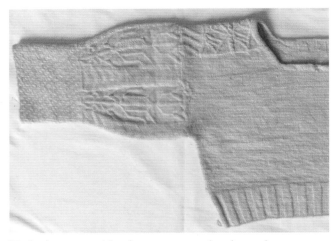

Undyed sweater with a few very unusual and complex patterns (FMN T013).

CONSTRUCTION

A night sweater most likely began with the sleeves, which were typically knitted from the cuff up. An edging was knitted first and then, most often, followed by traveling stitch and star motifs. The pattern repeats on many of the sweaters became wider and higher as they were increased, so there were no visible increases along a "sleeve seam."

The body was knitted from the bottom up and begun with edge pieces for the front and back, often in a block pattern or ribbing, knitted back and forth on two needles. After that, the two edges were joined and the body was then knitted in the round on anywhere between six and nine double-pointed needles. At the underarm, the piece was divided and the front and back worked separately, back and forth. The front and back necklines were sometimes straight across, sometimes rounded. The shoulders were worked straight up, one at a time and finished by joining with three-needle bind-off. Lastly, the sleeves were sewn in.

The Falster "shoulder seam" most often sat not directly on the shoulders, but somewhat forward. See, for example, this sweater from Karleby on Falster.

A sweater from Karleby. Here you can see how the front ends at the neck with a seam. (FMN 845/1914).

Here you can clearly see how the neckline continues out into the "shoulder seam" (FMN 845/1914).

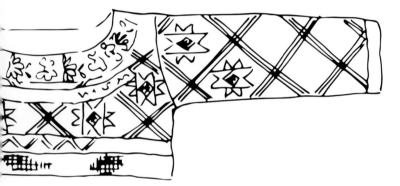

This sweater is 10 in / 25.5 cm long (shorter than a letter-sized piece of paper); the width is 11½ in / 29 cm (the same length as a letter-sized piece of paper).

Most of the sweaters that have been preserved are short (especially those from the beginning of the 19th century), and they're all very small by today's standards. The length varies from 9 to 13 in / 23 to 33 cm, and the width from 11¾ to 17¾ in / 30 to 45 cm. The length of the sleeves varies from three-quarters (the majority of the sweaters) to full arm length. Not many of today's adult women could shimmy their way into one of these sweaters. For the women of that time, however, they were quite practical. The chest was kept warm, and the sweaters could be quickly pushed up over the breast when women needed to breastfeed—not inconsequential for women who were in a constant cycle of giving birth and breastfeeding. People were also smaller in the past; the food was not as rich or varied as it is today.

SEATTLE SWEATER

Origin: Shoulder seams set at the front, which led me to immediately believe that the sweater was brought to the USA from Falster, Denmark.
Museum number: 2004.13.47.
Conserved in: Nordic Heritage Museum, Seattle, USA.

Measurements: C: 30¾ in / 78 cm; TL: 12¾ in / 32 cm; SL: 8¾ in / 22.5 cm
Color: Green.
Knitting gauge: 38 sts x 70 rows = 4 x 4 in / 10 x 10 cm.
Patterns: Vertical panels and edge patterns on the body. Traveling stitch and star motifs and edge patterns on the sleeves.

MISTAKES AND ERRORS?

My contemporary eyes caught many small errors and mistakes. They evidently weren't considered important—or perhaps the knitter simply didn't see them while knitting by the light of a fireplace, train-oil lamp, or small ring of candles. Increases on the body above the edge were most often placed arbitrarily and unsystematically, but it didn't matter, because they were usually invisible. I think these errors give the sweaters personality.

THE THREAD OF FATE, OR … ?

Many night sweaters have a little strand of thread hanging from the front edge. There aren't any other loose ends besides this one. In Skåne, Sweden, I found out that it used to be considered bad luck to finish something completely; perhaps that's the reason why this one last end wasn't woven in. However, it could also have been a thread of fate, which is a feature of Nordic mythology. The Norns—the fates, in other words—were thought to spin people's destinies, and each time one of their threads was cut, a person died. Better not to take a chance when the consequences are so serious.

FULLING AND WASHING

I have often heard that sweaters were fulled until they were almost disfigured after knitting, but I'm not sure that was entirely accidental. At one point in time, the Museum Lolland-Falster had three sweaters which belonged to the same woman, Maren Smed, from Aastrup on Falster—perhaps they were the only sweaters she owned. It's clear that the oldest is the one most fulled, the next not so much, but the third is in between. I think brand-new night sweaters were washed and fulled to soften them, though of course more fulling came from years of wear.

It isn't difficult to imagine what happened when sweaters were worn while one worked and sweated all day long. These sweaters were very seldom washed, and when that happened, it wasn't with wool-safe soap on a washing machine's wool cycle.

In the book *In the Footsteps of Our Mothers*, Helene Strange writes:

Before newly knitted sweaters were worn, they were supposed to be "fulled" on a fulling (or felting) board. Fulling boards were wood and similar to a wavy washboard. The wool garment was first washed and then fulled. It wasn't rubbed vigorously against the board, but lightly rolled up and down, so that the rolling movements would make the fabric soft, strong, and warm.
(From H. Strange, 1945).

However, at another place in the same book, we read that when washing wool garments, it was very important to do so carefully or the fabric could become hard as a board and shrink, thus making the garment unwearable.

It was hard work to do washing, especially in winter. Many washed with rainwater, which came down over thatch roofs before it was collected for washing—not especially clean, in other words. Others did the washing at the river, which was cleaner. Some people had their own wells, but there wasn't always sufficient water. Wool is self-cleaning to some degree, of course, but houses in the past were probably permeated with rather strong smells—and it was like that everywhere.

Maren Smed. Private photo.

THE COLORS OF THE SWEATERS

All of the night sweaters preserved in Denmark are made in a single color. They're mostly red and green, but some are black, or blue. The Lolland-Falster night sweaters I've examined break down into 28 green, 18 red, 13 black, and 1 white (undyed). However, it can be very difficult to determine whether a sweater was green, black, or blue, due to wear, washing, and the passage of time.

Red sweaters were mostly worn for going to town or church, but as they became worn out, they were consigned to everyday wear.

Ellen Andersen wrote in *The Danish Farmers' Costume* about 19th-century night sweaters:

Here and there in the country (North Zealand, Heden, Drejø, and other small islands), people remember that red night sweaters and skirts were worn until Whitsun, with green ones worn in the summer. It was green until Easter and in the spring, while blue sweaters were worn for Christmas and during the winter.
(From E. Andersen, 1960).

Some of the sweaters in the Museum Lolland-Falster are dark green, and very worn out and torn. On Falster, red sweaters were typically worn by younger women (unmarried), and green by older women. Perhaps so many of the green sweaters survived precisely because they were worn by old women, while younger women were quicker to adopt new styles of dress and discard their unfashionable night sweaters.

AASTRUP SWEATER

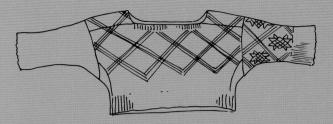

Origin: Aastrup, Falster.
Museum number: MLF 0521 x 001.
Conserved in: Museum Lolland-Falster.

Measurements: C: 33 in / 84 cm; TL: 11½ in / 29 cm; SL: 8¾ in / 22 cm.
Color: Dark green.
Knitting gauge: 37 sts = 4 in / 10 cm.

Patterns: Traveling stitch and edge patterns on the body. Traveling stitch and star motifs and edge patterns on the sleeves. Note the long stars on the sleeves.

HISTORY OF THE NIGHT SWEATER

OVERVIEW OF THE STYLES

It isn't easy to determine the age of night sweaters in museums. As a rule of thumb, you can take as a starting point that the longest sweaters, of which there are only a few, are the oldest and the short ones, the majority of what we find, are more recent. The short versions are from the period referred to as "Empire" style (approximately 1800-1825), and the long ones are from the period prior to that (from K. Gudmand-Høyer, 1995).

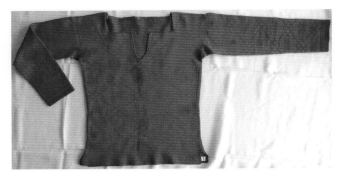

From the length of this sweater from Herning, we can surmise that it is from before 1800. It has particularly fine sleeve- and neck edgings with several braid rows.

I have the impression that the heyday of the knitted night sweater was in the first half of the 19th century; but it's entirely possible that that's only because most of the sweaters we have preserved are from that time. Night sweaters were also part of traditional folk costumes long before their heyday. The following citations tell us how early night sweaters were worn—even by the less well-off—and about when they went out of style.

SILK NIGHTSHIRTS (1600S AND 1700S)

In Maj Ringgaard's article, "An infant's silk knitted sweater from Lossepladsen," it's mentioned that night sweaters were already being worn in the latter part of the 17th century and were a common part of ordinary wardrobes for both rich and poor. Writings about Copenhagen traders give us clues about clothing, too.

In 1681, for example, the "Mohr Bargain Shop" sold to common citizens 58 fringed wool night sweaters for children from their stock, "the cheapest red (probably dyed with madder) and the most expensive nacarat (a red-orange dye from cochineal)," but "none of silk either for adults or children." Higher class shops where the more well-off people shopped supplied the much more expensive silk nightshirts in their stockrooms.

Leonora Christina, a famous Danish countess, was wearing a silk nightshirt when she was arrested in London in 1663. She was extradited to Copenhagen and imprisoned in the Blue Tower, where she had to relinquish her garment. In return, she later received "two night sweaters, one of knitted silk and one of white napped fabric." (*From www.askp.dk>Kvindens klædeskab>Nattrøje*).

WOOL NIGHT SWEATERS (1600S-1800S)

Mariann Ploug found evidence in a 17th-century Danish parish book revealing that wool night sweaters have been part of common Danish women's dress for nearly 400 years:

The priest in Vonsild relates that Cecilie Iversdatter, born in 1618 in Vildbjerg, Hammerum Herred, after the enemies had invaded the country, learned to knit wool night sweaters and, since that time, earned her living by it … until she married and moved to Vonsild.
(From M. Ploug, 1981).

A woman who, in 1762, fled from the jail in Ringsted, was described in a poster this way:

The person is of small stature, speaks Holstein Danish, and was dressed in a red vadmal vest, with green dyed wool sleeves, and a brown vadmal skirt, as well as wooden shoes on her feet. (From www.textilnet.dk).

From about the same period, more specifically in 1776, we find a story about Lolland by Peter Rhode. He describes the local dress this way:

The peasant's folk costume in Lolland is extremely simple, even among the wealthier independent farmers; except for a pair of boots every other year, or shoes, he doesn't spend more than 3 daler annually on his whole outfit, which consists of a white shift and a pair of leather or skin trousers. The costume of the farmer's wife, even here in North Herred where people are more prosperous, seldom consists of more than a bodice or sleeveless sweater, of homemade blue striped or linsey-woolsey fabric; a dark red, dyed, knitted sweater underneath; a shift or skirt of red bay [a thick, soft, light baize fabric] or rye [a rough woolen fabric]; and a cap of bought fabric.
(From P. Rhode, 1776, my emphasis).

Even in Hans Christian Andersen's fairytale, known in Danish as "Whatever Father Does, It Is Always Right," there are mentions of night sweaters:

'You always know what's best!' said the wife. 'You are always thoughtful; we have plenty of grass for a sheep. Now we can have sheep's milk and sheep's cheese and wool stockings, yes, even wool night sweaters! The cow doesn't provide any of that! She loses all her hair! You are such an amazingly thoughtful husband!'

DANISH NIGHT SWEATERS

HERNING SWEATER

Origin: Unknown.
Museum number: 20960.
Conserved in: Museum Midtjylland (Central Jutland).

Measurements: C: 33½ in / 85 cm TL: 21¼ in / 54 cm; SL: 17¼ in / 44 cm
Color: Red.
Knitting gauge: 43 sts = 4 in / 10 cm.
Patterns: Traveling stitch and star motifs, horizontal panels and edge patterns on the body. Traveling stitches and star motifs and edge patterns on the sleeves.

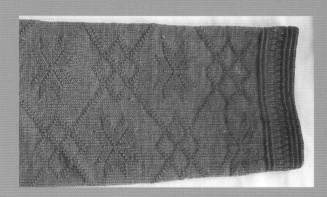

Helene Strange

Helene Strange (1874-1943) with her knitting. She was an author and collector of folk memorabilia. She wrote books and articles of invaluable significance for our knowledge about Falster traditions and about life in Falster's countryside in the past. Local History Association for North Falster.

BOUGHT CLOTHING (FROM THE MID-NINETEENTH CENTURY)

Helene Strange, an author from Falster, wrote that until at least the 1860s, all women, rich and poor, young and old, wore regional traditional dress. This outfit included a knitted night sweater, which was worn late into the 19th century. After that time, it was replaced by bought clothing.

The night sweater became old-fashioned and the style quite simply disappeared—young people were the first to give them up, followed by the older and less well-off.

On Falster there were still some of the older people and so-called *skørdekunner* who wore traditional skirts (part of the local traditional costume) into the 1900s. "Here on North Falster, there still lived (in 1918) about a dozen or so very old women who wore *skørd*," writes Helene Strange. The word *skørd* refers to the traditional regional dress. On Falster, the word for a purchased version of this garment was *kjoel* ("skirt").

She also relates that the old considered their youthful attire much nicer than modern outfits. "And it was something, nothing like the rubbish they wear now."
(From Toxværd et al, 1926).

On both Lolland and Falster, the night sweater was worn as part of standard local dress until both style and the economy in the last part of the 19th century made buying clothes more common. On North Falster, though, they proudly held fast to their traditional dress, much longer than in other places. That partly explains why it's on Falster that so many sweaters have been preserved.

NORTH ØRSLEV SWEATER

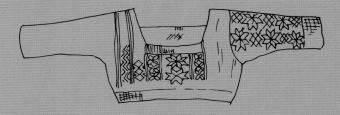

Origin: North Ørslev, Falster.
Museum number: LSF 7007.
Conserved in: Museum Lolland-Falster.

Measurements: C: 31½ in / 80 cm; TL: 11 in / 28 cm; SL: 9¼ in / 23.5 cm.
Color: Red.
Knitting gauge: 33 sts and 76 rows = 4 x 4 in / 10 x 10 cm.
Patterns: Stars at center front, vertical panels and edge patterns on the body. Traveling stitch and star motifs and edge patterns on the sleeves.

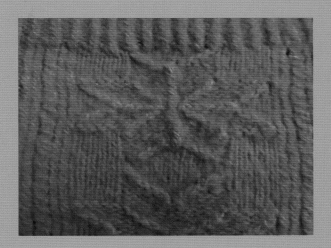

YARN AND NEEDLES

WOOL YARN

In describing the process of making night sweaters, it's important to begin at the beginning. The yarn would have been spun with wool from local sheep. First, after the sheep were shorn, the wool was cleansed of impurities, sorted, carded, spun, plied, and wound into balls, and only then could the knitting begin.

CARDING AND SPINNING

After the sheep were shorn and the wool washed, it was carded. Up until the middle of the 19th century, there were carding parties in the autumn on most farms to make this hard work more enjoyable. Later on, people carded at home or hired a woman to do the work so she could earn a bit of money. By the 1880s, this ceased, and instead wool was sent to town where it could be machine-carded.

After carding, the fiber was spun into yarn and then plied and wound into balls. Most of the spinning and plying was done on spinning wheels, but drop spindles were also in use because they were easy to carry around and could be used while walking or watching the herds. Hand tools were needed to produce yarn fine enough to reach a knitting gauge of, for example, 42 stitches and 80 rows in 4 x 4 in / 10 x 10 cm, which we can see on some of the finest sweaters in museum collections.

Later on, wool was sent to mills for spinning, which saved people a great deal of work.

WINDING YARN BALLS

People never wasted time, back then, and went nowhere without their knitting. Yarn was wound by hand into tight balls—often on a winding stick (*nøstepinne*) so the yarn could be pulled from the center of the ball, which was very practical when one wanted to walk and knit at the same time. The yarn ball was fastened to the clothing with a yarn hook, or simply held pinned under one arm by the knitter.

A winding stick was most often a gift from a beloved or husband. They were carved from wood, and could be decorated very intricately.

The knitter might also have her yarn ball in a little ball carrier, which meant drawing the yarn out through an eyehole in the ball. The ebony ball in the center left photo on the facing page could be worn around the wrist with a silk ribbon; not everyone was privileged enough to own such a fine item.

TOOLS

The big advantage of knitting is that it's relatively easy to turn out well-made, useful, and practical items with nothing but yarn and some needles—in contrast to weaving, which requires a much more complicated set-up. Knitting can also be done in the round; with weaving, you can only produce flat yardage/meterage.

Knitting needles from the period aren't easy to find. Knitting needles were made of wood, bone, or iron—or, if they were particularly fine, brass. Wood or bone needles were typically carved by a fiancé or husband, but needles could also be bought from traveling peddlers, at markets, or in shops in town.

When knitting in the round on, for example, a sweater body, several double-pointed needles were used, preferably six to eight needles to hold the stitches and one needle to knit with. Circular needles weren't available until long after night sweaters had gone out of fashion. I've seen indications that eight needles were used for a Danish night sweater, and six for stitches plus one to knit with on a Skåne sweater.

Another practical tool was a needle protector; these were made of various materials. The needle protector in the top photo on the facing page is silver, and shaped like very fine boots.

This winding stick with a little ball of yarn on it is particularly finely carved, with slots and a little ball inside. It could also serve as a rattle and entertain a baby in a cradle while yarn was wound.

DYEING

PLANT DYEING OR PIECE DYEING

As mentioned previously, night sweaters were first knitted with white wool yarn and then dyed. The sweaters were typically piece-dyed—that is, the finished garment was dyed at a dyehouse to avoid using more dyestuff than necessary. It's easy to understand why: it was more expensive to have fabric dyed than to have it woven.

It was common to use plant-dyed yarn for stripes for woven everyday skirts. So, you might wonder, why didn't people plant-dye knitting yarn to open up the option for knitting with several colors? They might well have wanted dyeing that was more uniform and even than could be achieved by plant-dyeing yarn by hand, or maybe the convenience of the "man-made" method appealed. Perhaps it was simply that no yarn should go to waste.

In the book *Pregle, binde og lænke* (three words meaning "knit"), Ann Møller wrote:

Everyday garments were usually not dyed. For stocking knitting, dyed yarn was saved for sections that would be visible under a skirt or trousers.
(From A. M. Nielsen, 1983).

This sweater is white on the lower section but I think the white was knitted on to make it longer, rather than to save dyed yarn. (LFS 00692).

DYEHOUSES

There were dyehouses around the country which took in fabric and knitting to be dyed. In a travel book from 1806 by the priest L. M. Wedel, he gives a report of the annual amount of textiles and knitted goods that were dyed in 2 dye houses in Maribo:

At the house and factory-Flid, we especially noted two families, particularly, two gentlemen, the dyers Ærreboe and Tvede; (...) Mr. Ærreboe [worked] with his wife tirelessly and diligently in all types of dyeing (...) annually took in during the course of the year 1802, 97,687 Alen (1 alen = 0.627 m or .685 yd) consisting of drill cloth, tabby, linsey-woolsey, blue checkered linen canvas, blue canvas; **of knitted fabrics such as sweaters and sleeves, he annually dyed 30 sweaters and 90 to 100 pairs of sleeves.** *In the year 1792, the other dyer, Mr. Tvede, also began dyeing homemade garments.*
(from L. M. Wedel, 1806, my emphasis).

The dyehouse in Stubbekøbing. The buildings from the two dyehouses in Mølle Street and Grønne Street are still there. The dyeworks themselves are no longer in existence.

The dyeworks were well-regarded and an experienced dyer could become a member of a dyers' guild and work towards running their own dye factory. In the 19th century, there were at least 3 dyeworks in Stubbekøbing: one on the corner or Farver Street/Mølle Street (active 1837-53), another on the corner of Bager Street/Sønder Street, and

a third on Grønne Street. A census from the time reveals that the master, journeymen, and apprentices all lived at the dyeworks. Unfortunately, there is no trace left of what was produced.

COPENHAGEN RED

You can read about colors in an article from 1826, "The Falster Costume, particularly the Women's Costume."

The red knitted sweater was dyed in Copenhagen and the color was called "Copenhagen red." Those dyed in Stub-bekøbing, were brown red. The green sweaters were very dark and it was hard to find any that were a somewhat lighter green, which seemed to be older than the dark ones. (From K. Toxværd et al, 1926).

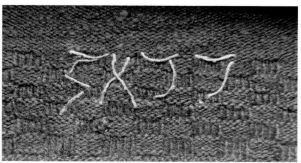

The name of the "Copenhagen red" color may have come from a dyeworks situated where Politikens Hus (home of the largest Danish newspaper) is today. It was located on a dyers' street right at the town gate. A person could drop off their garments before walking into town. Both garments and fabric were dyed there, and they also printed fabric with floral motifs. The dyeworks were established in 1727 and, after the dyer Jens Møller died, it was first continued by his widow, Engelke Møller, and then the master's loyal journeyman, Niels Holst, a professional.

EMBROIDERED NUMBERS

Most of the green sweaters (and a single red one) had large numbers embroidered with coarse linen thread on the sweater's lower edge. Obviously, they were embroidered before dyeing, and I surmise that it was the dye workers who sewed the numbers on. I'd hoped that the numbers indicated the color, owner, or something similar, but there was no evidence to support that. The numbers were apparently only numbers, corresponding to numbers in the dyers' system, so garments could be returned to the correct owner after dyeing.

DANISH NIGHT SWEATERS

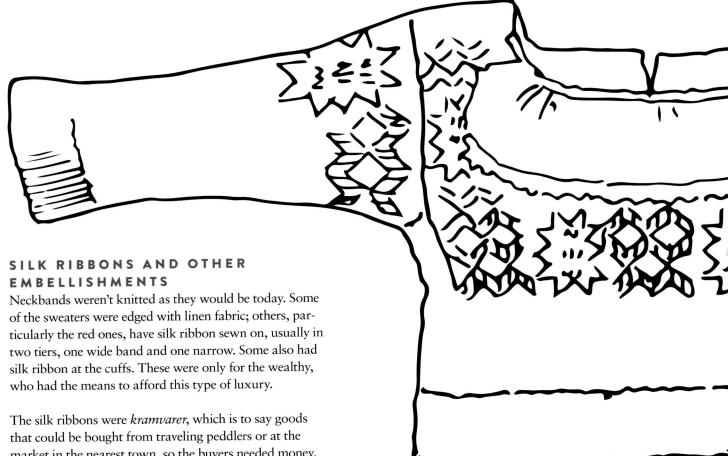

SILK RIBBONS AND OTHER EMBELLISHMENTS

Neckbands weren't knitted as they would be today. Some of the sweaters were edged with linen fabric; others, particularly the red ones, have silk ribbon sewn on, usually in two tiers, one wide band and one narrow. Some also had silk ribbon at the cuffs. These were only for the wealthy, who had the means to afford this type of luxury.

The silk ribbons were *kramvarer*, which is to say goods that could be bought from traveling peddlers or at the market in the nearest town, so the buyers needed money. Perhaps they were gifts to lovers? They were expensive, and there are clear signs that they were removed from older sweaters and sewn onto newer ones to save money.

It isn't surprising that silk ribbons were used to embellish red sweaters, because those were regarded as special "Sunday best" sweaters. Usually brides wore fine red knitted sweaters with silk ribbons as part of their bridal outfit. The bride would also have it on when she showed herself after the wedding night.

As decoration, silk scarves, lace, and silver buckles and clasps were also used, among other things. On Falster, people wore silk-decorated sleeves and *mamelukker* (Skåne sleeves).

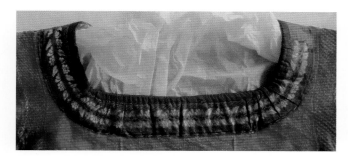

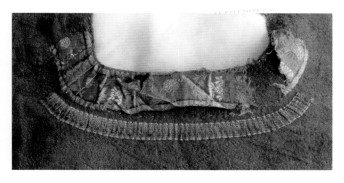

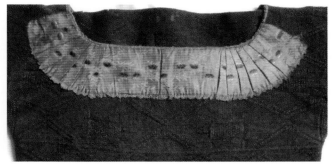

REGIONAL DISTINCTIONS AND CHARACTERISTICS

Among all the sweaters I researched, 45 came from Falster [1 in Seattle, USA, 11 from Lolland, 17 from various places in Zealand (Sjælland), 5 from Fyn, and 5 from Jutland (Jylland)—as well as 4 with unknown origin].

The little information available about any individual sweater usually focuses more on who donated the sweater to the museum than who owned or knitted it. I decided to list the place where a sweater was donated as "place of donation," unless otherwise stated.

In several parts of the country, very few sweaters have been preserved. There is so little basic information that it would be difficult to determine any regional characteristics. On Lolland-Falster, on the other hand, so many sweaters have been saved that it's possible to make certain generalizations. Still, no two sweaters are the same.

CHARACTERISTICS OF NIGHT SWEATERS FROM NORTH FALSTER

Here are what these night sweaters can reveal about the knitting process.

Body: On a typical sweater from the north part of Falster, a braid row is worked immediately after the cast-on (see page 68) and then a "pole" panel (that is, ribbing, most often knit 2, purl 2) was worked back and forth. The two edges were overlapped (see page 77), and the garment then continued in the round in stockinette approximately up to the underarms, sometimes with "random" increases for shaping. After that, the pattern, always symmetrical, is worked. A traveling stitch pattern appears on many of the Falster sweaters, so we can plausibly say it's a Falster specialty (it's seen in other areas, too, but much less often). Narrow vertical panels run up the sides and then there's typically a wide vertical traveling-stitch-and-star panel, ending with a narrow vertical panel and stockinette at the

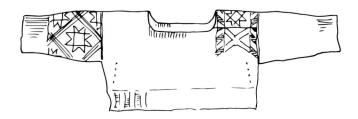

A typical sweater from Falster with traveling stitches. (FMN T071/1913).

center of the body. The neckline is often squared and made with a narrow ribbing.

The shoulders on the back are longer than the shoulder sections on the front. The shoulders are joined with three-needle bind-off—but not up on the shoulders. Many "shoulder seams" are aligned with the bind-off for the front neck. These sweaters have a small rounding of the front neck and "shoulder seams" directly above the rounding. Perhaps it was considered quite "smart." I imagine the

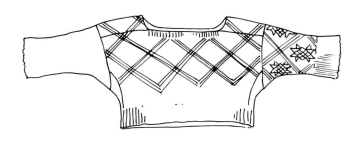

Shoulder seams align from the front of neck (MLF 0521 x 001, page 25).

Origin: Karlsfeldt, Stubbekøbing, Falster.
Museum number: FMN 3531a/1940.
Conserved in: Museum Lolland-Falster.

Measurements: C: 29¼ in / 74 cm; TL: 9 in / 23 cm; SL: 7 in / 18 cm.
Color: Red.
Knitting gauge: 51 sts and approx. 90 rnds = 4 x 4 in / 10 x 10 cm.
Patterns: A heart at the center front, vertical traveling stitch and star motifs; edge stitch patterning on the body. Traveling stitch and star motifs and edge patterns on the sleeves.

sleeves were worked first, and then the lower part of the body up to the division of back and front at the underarms. The front was completed next, and then the back was worked, with the shoulder sections adjusted to be long enough so the sleeves fit into the armholes well.

Birthe Nielsdatter from Hillestrup, Falster, dressed to the nines. Note that only the tops of the night sweater's sleeves are visible. Probably painted by Johannes Zehngraf. Falster's Memories, Museum Lolland-Falster.

Sleeves: The sleeves were worked from the top down on 4 needles. After the cast-on, there was usually a braid row and then an edging (ribbing, most often knit 2, purl 2 or knit 1 twisted, purl 1) and, finally, traveling stitch and star motifs. The increases were integrated into the traveling stitch and star patterns, which invisibly become larger and larger—a nicely sophisticated method of widening the sleeves. Sleeves ended with a little gusset below the underarm.

DISTINCTIVE CHARACTERISTICS OF NIGHT SWEATERS FROM SOUTH FALSTER

Sleeves: In south Falster, knitted sleeves were sewn onto a fabric body. These bodies were very beautifully worked, often with a peplum on the back.

There's such a big difference in the clothing styles of the north and south because each has its own history. In 1513, King Christian II "imported" some Dutch people to Amager and a few to Sprogø to cultivate the land. They were given special rights (not having to pay taxes was one of their privileges). The Dutch on Sprogø didn't take to the work, though, and in 1522 they (numbering 13 at the time) were granted permission to leave, first to sandy Bøtø on south Falster and then to lush Hasselø, a few kilometers south of Nykøbing, Falster. Here they cultivated vegetables for Nykøbing Castle, where the widowed Queen Sophie (1557-1631) lived. They continued going about in their own East Frisian outfits, but elements of their dress were gradually integrated into local clothing styles.

DISTINCTIVE CHARACTERISTICS OF NIGHT SWEATERS FROM LOLLAND

Few sweaters have been preserved from Lolland, so it's difficult to describe precisely how they looked, but we do have some information!

Body: On these sweaters, for example, one from Nysted (museum number LFS 14568), they are edged the same way those from Falster are edged (as here, with the block pattern) with a braid row often both before and after the edging. After that point, they were knitted in the round. (See pattern on page 208).

A horizontal panel is often knitted above the edging—for example, a zigzag—and then traveling stitch and star patterns cover the rest of the sweater, although there could be vertical side panels or gussets. The neck shaping was most often covered by a fine silk ribbon on the right side and sometimes an additional linen lining on the underside.

Sleeves: The cast-on was often followed by a braid row, and then an edge pattern (most often ribbing), and then traveling stitch and star motifs with increases integrated into the patterning.

THE REST OF THE WARDROBE FROM FALSTER AND LOLLAND

Under night sweaters people wore knee-length shifts with undershirts over them. Both of these garments were made of canvas linen and could be sleeved or sleeveless.

Over the night sweater was a bodice, the earliest of which had long skirts and fitted closely up to the neck; later versions had short skirts and a deeper neckline. The bodice closed at the front with a pin (*knappenåle*), hooks and eyes, or with eyelets of silver rings and ties with a silver pin in each end.

On the lower body, over the shift, one wore one or more skirts of vadmal or linsey-woolsey (woven with a linen warp and wool weft). Later came padded cotton skirts. One's dignity certainly froze because there was nothing under the skirt (underpants weren't common yet!). In the winters, one might wear a leather skirt, that is, a skirt of sheep's skin with the wool side facing in (with fur and all), edged with vadmal at the lower front.

On the feet, people wore knitted stockings and wooden shoes or slippers—or, for special occasions, fine leather shoes.

WHY WERE NIGHT SWEATERS FROM FALSTER SO HIGHLY REGARDED?

Several places in Denmark where I have researched night sweaters at museums have particularly beautiful examples, but the most artful were the Falster sweaters. Many of them were beautifully designed with damask patterns, some with traveling stitches, braid rows, and fine details.

It was especially important for a young woman to be able to show off her finest night sweater at her wedding, so her husband's family could see that a skilled woman was coming into the household.

Traveling stitches are a special knitting technique, which I've also seen outside of Denmark. They appear on gloves from Runö (an island off the coast of Estonia). This island is known for its special and artistically-made gloves with traveling stitches. This technique has also embellished sweaters from Austria, where even now there is a tradition of knitting sweaters with vertical traveling stitch panels. We don't know whether this kind of pattern reached Denmark by being brought home as a knitted "souvenir" from a trip aboard a ship from the east, or perhaps by carriage after a trip in Europe, but it's fascinating to think about.

Part of the credit for beautiful Danish handwork, especially on Falster, can also be ascribed to the sewing schools established in the 19th century. General Major and landowner J. F. Classen, who owned the Corselitze property on Falster in 1768-92, was a very rich man, and he had no heirs. He wished that, after his death, his fortune should be used to better the conditions of the local peasants, including their education. One of the measures undertaken as a result was the establishment of sewing schools in the country towns on North Falster. The first was founded in 1822. Instructors were hired, housing was set up, and heating and a little money arranged so girls could be taught handcrafts. The schools continued to function for a long time, so even today we can find Falster women who were taught there. I'd imagine that these sewing schools helped girls in the area become especially skilled at handwork.

A sewing school in Moseby. Photo from 1914. The girls wearing white aprons sit with their knitting while some crochet or work embroidery. Stubbekøbing Local History Archive.

KNITTED HANDWORK

KNITTING HISTORY

Knitting is relatively new compared to handcrafts like sewing and weaving—only about a thousand years old. We don't know where it originated. There isn't much knowledge about its origins but there are some clues from a few preserved items.

IN EUROPE

The supposition that knitting might have come to Spain via Arabic influence is supported by knitted silk pillows with which the Spanish king Ferdinand de la Cerda was buried in 1275. The pillows are knitted at a gauge of 80 stitches in 4 in / 10 cm. They have Islamic design elements, so one might imagine that they were knitted by a very skillful Arabic knitter. From there, knitted handwork probably continued its wandering up through Europe.

It wasn't long before European bishops began wearing knitted liturgical gloves. These gloves were very artfully worked. The gloves in the picture below were probably from Spain, but more of this type of glove can be found in several European museums.

Liturgical gloves from the sixteenth century, knitted with red silk yarn and gold thread. The top of the hand has about 85 stitches across the front, for a total of 170 sts around, which is an exceedingly fine gauge. Victoria and Albert Museum, London.

On several altarpieces, pictures of the Madonna show her not only knitting, but knitting in the round, a concept worth noting. We can conclude that knowledge of circular knitting was already common around the middle of the 14th century, as these paintings show.

In northern Europe, the oldest knitting finds are from Schleswig around 1150. A fragment of a wool mitten or glove in multicolored knitting (white, red, and blue) was found in a grave from about 1300 in Estonia.

The Madonna of Tommaso da Modena, 1325-79.

The altarpiece was painted in about 1345. Note the Madonna knitting in the round.
Pinoteca Nazionale di Bologna (The National Art Gallery of Bologna), Bologna, Italy.

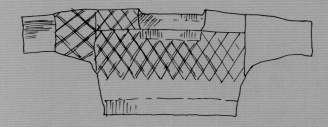

Origin: Kraghave, Falster
Museum number: FMN 2792/1930.
Conserved in: Museum Lolland-Falster.

Measurements: C: 30¼ in / 77 cm; TL: 11 in /
28 cm; SL: 7 in / 18 cm.
Color: Black.
Knitting gauge: 52 sts and 80 rows = 4 x 4 in /
10 x 10 cm.
Patterns: Traveling stitch and edge patterns
on the body and sleeves.

KNITTING GUILDS

Eventually knitting became a profession with master teachers. By 1268, the first guild had been established in Paris. Later, journeymen in Spain, Italy, and Germany organized into guilds and churches, and the nobility could order knitted goods from these master knitters.

Knitting was considered men's work and acquired esteem. After a long training period of 6-7 years, their education was concluded with a professional piece. Once these pieces were approved by the guild's master, the student had completed his training. The Victoria and Albert Museum in London has one such professional piece, a carpet from Strasbourg dated 1781. It was knitted with very fine needles (perhaps on a frame) with many colors, and it's very detailed and rich with motifs.

ELASTIC STOCKINGS

One of the reasons that knitted clothing became so popular was because, in contrast to sewn stockings, knitted stockings were flexible and elastic—which constituted a revolutionary development, for stockings.

At the same time as men's knee breeches came into fashion in the 16th century, knitted stockings also became stylish—or perhaps trousers became shorter in order to show off the stockings. And they were certainly worth showing off, because they were not only attractive but also unbelievably expensive. For example, the fashion-conscious King Erik XIV (1533-77) of Sweden imported silk stockings. The stockings cost him as much as his chamber servants earned in a year (which also tells us how bad conditions were for chamber servants). The cost meant that the stockings were repaired even if owned by men of noble descent.

Elizabeth I, Queen of England from 1558 to 1603, is likely the first woman to have worn knitted stockings. It is worth noting that she made her influence felt so powerfully that knitting became women's work.
(From *Gyldendals Sewing and Knitting Book*, 1940).

NOBLE NIGHTSHIRTS

King Charles I of England is said to have worn a distinctive sky-blue silk knitted nightshirt when he was beheaded in the Tower of London on January 30, 1649. It was a bitterly cold day. Rumor had it that the king asked that he be allowed to keep his nightshirt on so he would avoid shivering from the cold. He didn't want people to think he was shaking like a coward. The garment was knitted in the round in single-color damask knitting. The king's doctor took the nightshirt and it remained in his family's possession until it was donated to the Museum of London, where it is now conserved.

Night sweaters (which is what silk knitted nightshirts came to be called in Scandinavia) were in fashion among the well-to-do. Most of these sweaters were a single color, knitted with knit and purl stitches in well-recognized and popular diamond and star motifs which I call "traveling stitch and star" patterns. Many of these sweaters also had richly arranged silver or gold embroidery. We don't know whether they were knitted in Scandinavia, in the countries south of Denmark, or perhaps in England, but we do know that they were very beautiful and expensive, and therefore not only worn at night.

The characteristic traveling stitch and star patterns on these fine imported silk sweaters were the inspiration for the woolen night sweaters worn by peasants. However, the wool sweaters developed their own style.

HANDWORK FOR EVERYONE

Knitting guilds produced complex creations for the nobility, but of course knitting eventually became an everyman's—or everywoman's—method of handwork. All that was needed was yarn, a pair of knitting needles, and a lot of diligence and patience. That it's easy to knit while walking, sitting, and standing, and that knitting projects are so portable, contributes to the spread of knitting and its popularity even today.

IN DENMARK

Maj Ringgaard wrote this about Denmark's history of knitting:

It is generally thought that knitting came from Jutland to the islands. In Schleswig, some knitted fabric had been

A red silk knitted nightshirt with gold embroidery from Oslo. The shirt was likely knitted outside Scandinavia. Norwegian Museum of Cultural History, Oslo.

found with other rags, recycled in a type of broom or padding dated back to 1150. The first Danish written mention of knitting is from the middle of the sixteenth century, where knitted socks are mentioned in a pair of letter exchanges from the same period when a knitted cap or beret was found in Copenhagen. In Bergen—then part of the Danish-Norwegian kingdom—knitted fragments were found in earth layers from around the year 1500. (From private correspondence).

A special tube-shaped silver item at the National Museum of Denmark points in the same direction. This item is called a "knitted sheath"—it's a tool used to support knitting needles (similar to the way people on the Shetland Islands use a knitting belt). It bears the inscription "Ellin Glambek." She was married to Albert Vind (1543-1608), of the Ullerup Estate on Mors. This allows us to confirm that knowledge of knitting had already come into Denmark by Ellin Glambek's time period, at least among the upper classes. (Fra L. Warburg, 1980).

A passage from a letter to Birgitte Bølle (later Gøye) from Christoffer Gøye in 1566 adds further support to the assertion that knitting was in Demark by the middle of the 16th century. He writes:

The womanly youth before learning to knit and work sprang; they first were diligent at sewing, but now they are learning to knit.
(From I. L. Pedersen, 1987).

In Jutland, home industry (including knitting) was seriously underway by 1630. The priest and author St. St. Blicher wrote in 1839 in the book *Viborg County* that peasant knitting for sale in the parishes of Lysgaard and Hammerrum went further back than anyone could remember or has written about.

Mette Marie Jensdatter from Sundby on Mors with her "stocking knitting." From the book Old Springs. *(E. T. Kristensen, 1981), Danish Folk Memories at The Royal Library.*

KNITTED HANDWORK

KØGE SWEATER

Origin: Unknown.
Museum number: T359.
Conserved in: Køge Museum.

Measurements: C: 31 in / 79 cm; TL: 11 in / 28 cm; SL: 11½ in / 29 cm.
Color: Dark blue.
Knitting gauge: 40 sts = 4 in / 10 cm.
Patterns: Traveling stitch and star motifs; edge patterns on the body. Traveling stitch and star motifs and vertical panels on the sleeves. Note the vertical panel widens with increases as it goes up the sleeve.

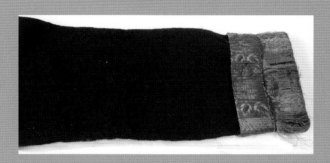

MANY WORDS FOR KNITTING: *LÆNKE, PREGLE, BINDE, KNYTTE, STRIKKE*

The word *strikke* is used in Denmark today to describe the process of knitting, no matter what method is used. It was different in the 19th century. The action of knitting was named with several different words in the dialects and regions of the country, and knitting methods also differed around the country.

THE SAME HANDWORK—SEVERAL WORDS

lænke was the word used for knitting on Lolland, Falster, Bogø and the western half of Møn and on the most southern part of Zealand;

pregle was used in south and southwest Jutland;

knytte was a word common to many places; and,

binde was the word found in the larger areas of Jutland, on Fyn, and Zealand, or anywhere else *lænke*, *pregle*, and *knytte* weren't used.

The dialect scholar Inge Lise Pedersen states that the word *lænke* was used as far back as 1647, and it referred to the knitting method of that time: right-hand knitting (R-knitting) one stitch at a time (see page 56). (From I. L. Pedersen, 1988).

Helene Strange relates that people on Falster said *lænke* until, in the 1870s, they shifted to left-hand knitting (L-knitting). In this case, the word is also linked to the method. In her 1945 book *In Our Mothers' Footsteps*, she wrote:

Also, women should and could "lænke." Lænkning was the most old-fashioned method of knitting, in which the yarn was thrown over the needle with the right hand. By the end of the 1870s, knitters switched to the "forward" method, holding the yarn, as is done now, over the left index finger. In the transition, it was "most elegant" to say "strikke" instead of "lænke."
(From H. Strange, 1945).

When the dictionary states that *binde* was used to refer to the method "peasant wives" knitted with (see pages 47 and 56), it's a truth with qualifications, because Jutland knitters knitted as we do today, with the yarn on the left-hand index finger; it was faster, and people knitted to put bread on the table. They only used the word *binde*.

WHAT YOU'LL FIND IN DICTIONARIES OF THE DANISH LANGUAGE

Binde: *a linked thread of knots, loops, stitches, netting, etc; to knit (…)* "among peasants, it is about the same as to knit (strikke). But the farmer's wives used another finger arrangement for knitting (referred to as knytningen) as practised by the people from Kjøbstad. The word binde signifies = to knit like a peasant wife."

Knytte: *linked, braided, or knitted thread forming knots, loops, stitches, etc; also about knitting (…). Some knitted stockings, provided good warmth against frost (…) silk knitted shirts.*

Lænke: *forming (a thread, a cord) to a bow or loop (stitch); to knit, (…) If men all around had nothing else to do, they preferred to knit (binde) stockings or to knit (lænke) as it is called in common language. (…) The mother (sat) on the doorstep and knitted (lænkede) on a long white stocking.*

Pregle: *from prickeln, specifically: to knit (by a certain method) or to sew, embroider.*

Strikke: *Supercedes high Danish in some areas - a newer technique—the words such as binde, knytte. (…) producing stitches of yarn (wool, cotton, thread, silk) with the help of 2 or 4 (5) needles such that the yarn forms the loops from one to the other without a break; also, knitting (knitwear) produced on a knitting machine.*

TOREBY SWEATER

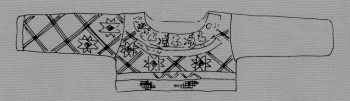

Origin: Toreby, Lolland.
Museum number: LFS 23885a.
Conserved in: Museum Lolland-Falster.

Measurements: C: 30¾ in / 78 cm; TL: 10 in / 25.5 cm; SL: 12¼ in / 31 cm.
Color: Red with silk ribbons.
Knitting gauge: 34 sts = 4 in / 10 cm.
Patterns: Traveling stitch and star motifs, horizontal panel and edge patterns on the body. Traveling stitch and star motifs and edge pattern on the sleeves.

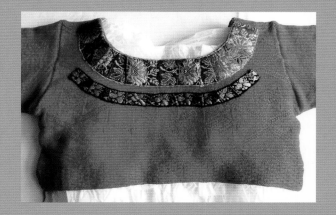

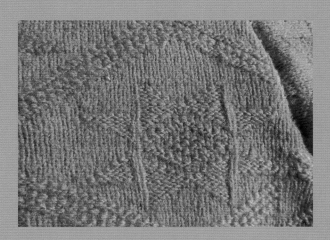

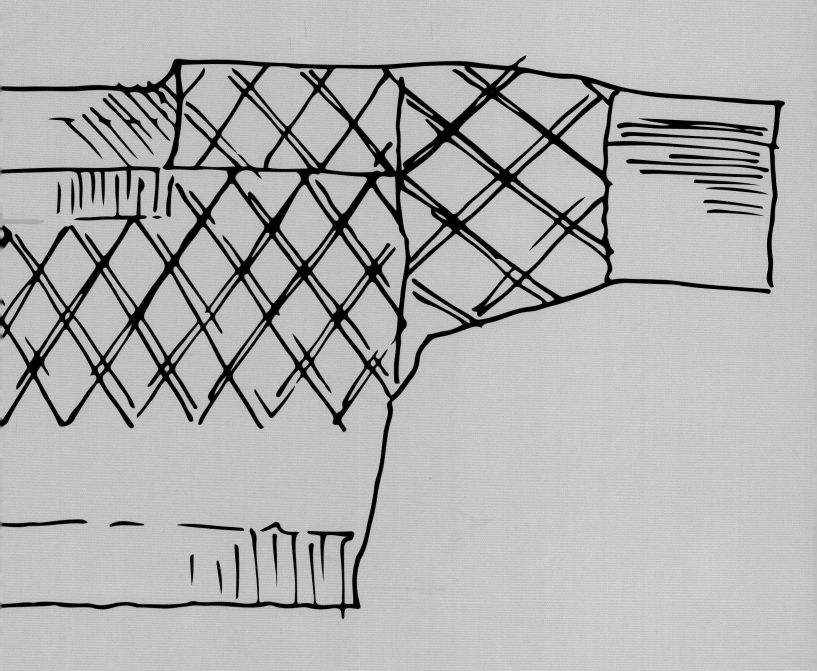

CONFUSION IN ROYAL LANGUAGE: WAS KNITTING FORBIDDEN?

I found the following in *Gyldendal's Sewing and Knitting Book* from 1940:

In the following year, interest in knitted clothing items was, in general, at such a level in Denmark and King Christian IV so opposed such beguiling luxury in the year 1636 that he felt obliged to issue a decree, **Restrictions against Knitted Items**, *to inform the people about who alone was allowed to obtain such goods. From then on, no non-noble women could wear silk stockings. The wives and daughters of the mayor and councilors, could, with special permission, wear wool stockings, but wives and daughters of common citizens and handworkers should under no circumstances go about wearing knitted stockings.* (My emphasis)

One might come to the conclusion that Christian IV wanted to stop the development of knitting. However, that was not the case. The explanation lies in Danish terminology. The word *strikke* (knit) comes from the German word *stricken*, which was used at that time to refer to finer,

finished knitted goods, predominantly imported products. Later, the word was used in relation to the merchandizing of knitted goods.

Christian IV didn't want to stop people from knitting—quite the opposite. In 1605, he actually instigated the building of a Disciplinary and Children's Home at Christianshavn, where orphaned children could learn various professions, including production knitting. The goal was for them to learn a profession they would later use. Perhaps Christian IV also had it in the back of his mind that knitting could be produced in Denmark to avoid excessively expensive importation of knitted goods. The institution existed until 1649.

In other places, some knitted goods were referred to as *bundne* ("bound") goods—this term was used to refer to home-knitted wool goods. So even if people were forbidden to go around in "knitted" stockings, they could still wear "bound" stockings, so to speak.

DANISH HANDWORK IN THE 19TH CENTURY

By the 19th century, knitting had spread throughout Denmark and it was quite common to knit. Paintings (and later photographs) from that period show women with their knitted garments. The typical portrayal was of country women with coarse knitted garments (such as socks), and wealthier women from the towns wearing fine white knitted clothing. (See the pictures on pages 58-59).

That which is done with the hands brings forth the spirit!

WHO KNITTED?

In the district of Jutland, where farming was sufficient to give families an adequate living, knitting offered a more stable source of income. Both sexes knitted here, and all ages, from young children to the oldest, unless blindness, physical impairment, or another illness prevented it. In the book *Spinning and Knitting*, H. P. Hansen wrote that the knitting industry played a large role for over 200 years, both because the poorest sector of the population earned their food from it and because the remaining population could be provided with knitted goods from this district. Blicher wrote in his book *Viborg County* (1839) that approximately 40,000 people were employed through knitting, and in many places knitting was the primary source of income.

Girls and married women were the knitters on the islands, including Lolland and Falster. For young girls in the countryside, knitting filled the hope chest and provided garments (fabric and night sweaters) for the young woman. When a girl was first married, she wouldn't have much time to make clothing for herself because she had the task of making clothes for her husband, children, and servants. These garments were strong, long-wearing, and repeatedly repaired.

When the work day was over, the knitting (or other handwork) came out, and as long as it was possible to see by daylight, girls and women knitted for their own use (for the hope chest); but once the candles were lit, girls did handwork for their mistress.

PLEASURE OR NECESSITY?

I imagine that most night sweaters were knitted by the women who wore them—or by local women who could earn a little by knitting for others. These sweaters shared certain local characteristics, but each was different and very much personal in its details.

If you look more closely at traditional night sweaters, many almost glow with knitting pleasure and knowledge

A Jutland Shepherd on the Heath, 1855, by Frederik Vermehren (1823-1910). The herder holds the yarn over his left index finger. State Museum of Art.

(for example, the North Ørslev sweater shown on the lower left of this page), while others imply that knitting was pure torture (for example, the Sønder Alslev sweater directly below). Some were harmoniously designed and elegant, while others have an almost random or impulsive arrangement of patterns, even when tradition is taken into consideration.

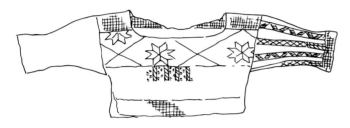

This sweater is from Sønder Alslev on Falster (FMN 102.5a). It has quite a mixture of motifs, and the neckline is uneven. Perhaps whoever knitted it hated to knit or only toyed with the work.

This sweater is clearly a masterpiece (LFS 7007, page 29). Both the design and knitting are excellent.

RIBE SWEATER

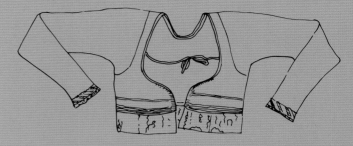

Origin: Tanderupgård, Ribe, Jutland.
Museum number: ASR M8386, 8393.
Conserved in: Sydvestjyske Museer (Southwest Jutland Museums).

Measurements: C: 34 in / 86 cm; TL: 13½ in / 34.5 cm; SL: 16½ in / 42 cm.
Color: Red with fabric sewed on at the neck and front lower edge.
Knitting gauge: approx. 36 sts = 4 in / 10 cm.

Patterns: Stockinette with a little garter stitch on the body. Stockinette with edge patterns on the sleeves.

In her article "Stocking Knitting" ("*Husselænkning*"), Helene Strange described knitting as a pleasant diversion:

For the most part, knitting was beloved and easy work, which, in the old days, women relaxed with as it was something that could be fitted in between other activities. They knitted when they rode by wagon, whether driving into town or out in the countryside, taking the occasion to get on with their work. Girls always had their knitting with them when they walked to the dairy. They carried milk in large jugs on their heads and, after they filled the jugs, they got out their stocking knitting and walked proudly back home with their fingers deftly clicking the knitting needles.

Knitting was practical handwork which could be done while sitting, standing, or walking. It was a welcome way of passing the time while walking, like the shepherd in the painting on page 50.

One of my great-grandmothers, Kirstine Marie (1844-1933), a widow with 5 children, was photographed while walking the 6.8 miles / 11 km from Bjerre Skov to Horsen to attend her oldest child's confirmation. Her wooden shoes hung around her neck (she was trying not to put too much wear on them) and she was working on her knitting. Idle hands were not well-regarded.

Correspondingly, St. Blicher mentions in *Viborg County* that there were many who knitted all the way to the

Tyge Slavig (my cousin) painted this picture of our great-grandfather, the wool merchant Niels Christian Hansen (1842-1891), who drove around selling woolen goods. At the beginning, he carried his goods on his back but later he had a horse and wagon. It was hard work that led to his early death. (With permission of Tyge Salvig.)

church door and again immediately on leaving the church after the service on Sundays or feast days.

Blicher also wrote about young men and women of the district who often gathered in the evenings in farm rooms transformed into knitting cottages. Here they vied to see who could knit the fastest and the most, played various games, sang, and told stories. These evenings were an enjoyable way to relax after a hard work day.

WOOL MERCHANTS

People knitted stockings, socks, underdresses (*klokker*), mittens, sleeves for men, and night sweaters, most of which were made to sell—except shawls, which were seldom for sale. The knitted wool garments were either for export— many were sent to Copenhagen, others to Holsten—or they were bought by wool dealers, like, for example, my great-grandfather, the wool merchant N. C. Hansen (1842-1891). He traveled around various parts of the country to sell woolen goods. From a late letter to his wife (1886), you can deduce from his complaints that townspeople no longer bought so freely. That was no surprise: by that point, there were trains, and towns were expanding by leaps and bounds with shops offering goods to buy. (From 15 years of letters in the possession of the family; the last is from 1889.)

ODENSE SWEATER

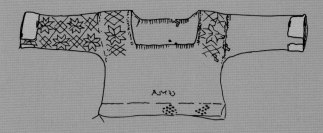

Origin: Sankt Hans, Odense, Fyn.
Museum number: KMO/1963/613.
Conserved in: Odense City Museum.

Measurements: C: 31½ in / 80 cm; TL: 13½ in / 34.5 cm; SL: 9½ in / 24 cm.
Color: Red.
Knitting gauge: 42 sts = 4 in / 10 cm.
Patterns: Vertical traveling stitch and star motifs, initials (AMD) and edge stitches on the body. Traveling stitch and star motifs on the sleeves.

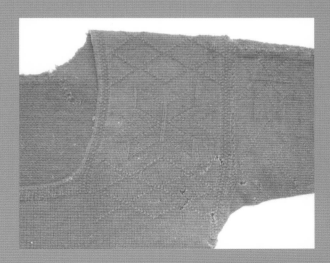

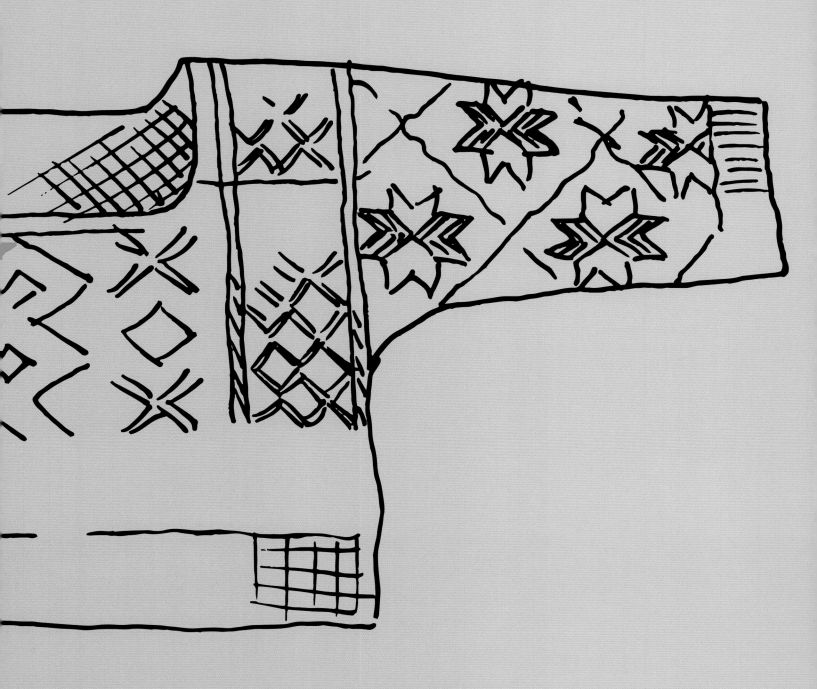

Hanne's
KNITTING SONG

Song from 1790.
In English, the rhythm and rhymes are lost; but the Danish
original was sung.

Certainly no Amazon
The first stocking knitted:
Nay, a young Nordic woman
The honorable art invented.
When tenderly she looked and saw,
That the dear little lasses froze.

She took up five needles,
And threw the loops on,
And from the wool twirling
Two stockings soon evolved.
She said: Wait little one!
Put your legs in here!

Then the mother smiled happily;
These stockings warmed so well;
With immense energy
She such warmth gave.
Soon the men had stockings to wear:
And lastly she herself had a pair.

Peace to the unknown Woman,
She will certainly live in heaven;
For from her knitting needles
Came Usefulness so great;
Now everyone who walks
about,
Has knitted stockings on.

Isn't it so amusing
With a skein held at your
bosom
Stockings for yourself to knit
And work to earn your bread!
What a poorly fated man,
Whose bride knows not how
to knit.

P. H. Haste

THREE KNITTING METHODS

You can find knitting in many, many places around the world, but knitting methods differ. In Denmark, for the most part, we all knit with the yarn held over the index finger of the left hand: left-hand knitting (L-knitting). In many places, this method is called the "continental method."

Danish women (at least those of us who are a little older), learned L-knitting thanks to Emilie West (1844-1907). She wrote *The Guidebook to Methodical Instruction in Women's Handwork* in 1889. It was immediately adopted by the schools and so we all learned to knit the same way. It worked so we didn't consider other methods. Because we all knit the same way, discussions about knitting were easier.

But what was the actual situation in the 19th century? From Eilert Sundt, a Norwegian folk life researcher, we find out that there were three different methods for knitting, the current left-hand style and two right-hand methods. He saw all three knitting methods demonstrated at a rectory, by both the priest's wife and daughter, and by a peasant girl who worked there. They each had their own way of holding the yarn and needles. Sundt described the three methods as follows:

1. A RIGHT-HAND METHOD (R-KNITTING)

The servant girl knitted a stitch this way:

She held the lower end of the knitting needle and inserted the tip into the stitch, let go of the needle, and lifted her arm and hand up to bring the yarn around the tip. (From E. Sundt, 1867).

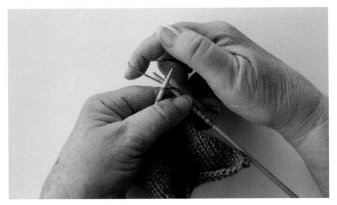

R-knitting with the yarn in the right hand and a stitch in progress.

Girl from Refsnæs at Kalundborg. She is knitting with the R-knitting method with a stitch in progress. Drawing by Frederik Christian Lund (1826-1901).

2. ANOTHER RIGHT-HAND METHOD (R-KNITTING, THE ENGLISH WAY)

The priest's wife knitting a stitch by the second method:

She held the needle high up and didn't release her hold. With the yarn lying on the index finger of the right hand, she threw it around the needle tip using only the movement of her fingers.
(From E. Sundt, 1867).

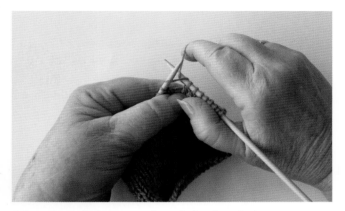

R-knitting with the yarn in the right hand, with the yarn remaining in the hand so that one stitch can be knitted after the other without dropping the work.

Painting by Julius Exner: An old sailor knitting a stocking—and it looks like he is using this second method, also called R-knitting or the English method. Exhibited at the Charlottenborg Spring Exhibition in 1898. Photographed in connection with the Vilh. Tillge.

3. A LEFT-HAND METHOD (L-KNITTING)

The priest's daughter knitted a stitch the third way:

She held the needles as for the previous method but had the yarn lying over the left-hand index finger. She inserted the needle tip through the stitch, caught the yarn from above and then brought it down and through to complete the stitch. (From E. Sundt, 1867).

L-knitting with the yarn over the index finger of the left hand and stitches worked one after the other.

Ane Margrete Hansen (born 1854), Havlund, knitting with the yarn over the left hand's index finger. From the book Old Springs. *(E. T. Kristensen 1981.) Danish Folk Memories at the Royal Library.*

EACH METHOD HAS ITS OWN PROPONENTS

When comparing the three knitting methods, we find that each has its own advantages.

With the first and second, it's the knitter's tension on the yarn (and, of course, the needle and yarn sizes), that determines the knitting gauge. One can, without any big problem, knit with inelastic yarns like cotton and silk. The third method requires an elastic yarn, and it's hard to knit firmly with this method.

When we knit with our contemporary method (L-knitting/continental), it's easy to see by the finished work if it was knitted in the round or flat (back and forth), because our purl rows are often looser than the knit rows. This can be seen on the work's wrong side because the ridges lie in pairs. By contrast, using the R-knitting method there are no row pairs, and so no difference between the right and wrong sides.

The second method was clearly developed by clever knitters who naturally adjusted the first method so their hands could continually knit stitch after stitch without releasing the needles, thus speeding up the work.

Joachim Junge (priest and author, 1791-1823) wrote about a woman knitting in Zealand (R-knitting):

Her knitting method led to wasting time: while others (here the author is thinking of people from Fyn) lay the yarn over the left hand's index finger, so as to pick the stitches up and off, she threw the yarn around the needle with her entire right hand.
(From J. Junge, 1798).

The Hirschsprung Family, painted by P. S. Krøyer in 1881. The Hirschsprung Collection. The picture shows an ideal presentation of a happy family. It also portrays the women engaged in their handwork. Ellen knits with the L-method and her mother is also knitting with the yarn over her lefthand index finger.

As regards the speed of knitting, Sundt asked one of the priest's daughters and a skilful farm girl to knit in competition. The result was that the priest's daughter knitted 70 stitches per minute while the farm girl could achieve no more than 30 stitches in a minute. The quickest method was the third (L-knitting) and the slowest was the first (R-knitting).

St. Blicher also tested the speed of knitting with the Jutland method (L-knitting):

This method, which these knitters all use, has the yarn held over the index finger of the left hand, which contributes greatly to the speed of knitting. The way the yarn goes from the hand makes it possible to knit a complete pair of men's stockings in two days when there is no other work. (From Blicher, 1839).

Portrait of Madam Schmidt painted by C. W. Eckersberg in 1818. The Hirschburg Collection. The East Indian merchant's wife knitting a stocking. Note that she holds the yarn over her righthand index finger, in the English method.

The first Danish knitting book was published in 1845: *The Knitting Book for Schools and Household Use* by Sine Andresen. It describes how to cast on but not how to knit. You can read about that in the *Instructor's Book on Women's Handwork* from 1875. Bite your tongue while you try this:

Using one of the methods given here, cast on the required number of stitches for the item and begin knitting.

Hold the needle with the cast-on stitches in the left hand and lay the yarn over the index finger of the left hand so that it can be held fast with the next finger. Take the other needle in the right hand, insert it from below up through the stitch, catch the yarn held around the index finger and bring it through the stitch. Now lift the finished stitch off the left needle—and the first stitch is now complete.

Continue until all the stitches have been worked onto the right needle; the empty needle now moves to the right hand and you can continue knitting from the other needle the same way.

Special
KNITTING TECHNIQUES

CAST-ONS

Before you begin to knit, you have to cast on. All cast-on methods start with one or two beginning stitches. According to the Instructor's Book of Women's Handwork *from 1875, (where the old drawing on page 64 comes from), you begin with two stitches. The following stitches can be cast on in several ways.*

When I studied the old night sweaters, I became very curious about how the women who knitted them cast on, knitted, etc. Unfortunately, there is no one from the nineteenth century to tell us, so I turned to the books from that era that I have on my book shelves. They are, respectively, *The Knitting Book for Schools and Household Use* by Sine Andresen from 1845 and the *Instructor's Book of Women's Handwork* published by Carl Aller's Publishing and Printing in 1875. These books were certainly not to be found in farmhouses where the night sweaters were knitted but we do find descriptions of the period's various methods for casting on and knitting in them.

The oldest Danish knitting book, with Gothic lettering, published patterns for practical items such as a swaddling wrap, a man's night cap, a bed cover, a shawl, a muff, etc.

BEGINNING STITCHES

ONE BEGINNING STITCH

Make the first stitch with simple slip knot. That's the way I learned in school.
It's the stitch that begins with a pretzel shape.

Hold the yarn tail to the right and the working yarn to the left.
Insert the left thumb from behind and below the yarn and form
a loop with the yarn end hanging down. Hold the loop with the
right hand and push the working yarn diagonally up through the
loop; insert the needle under the diagonal strand.

Pull the ends to tighten. There is now 1 stitch on the needle.

TWO BEGINNING STITCHES

This is a good method to begin with, and it doesn't make a knot.

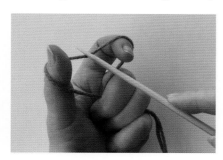 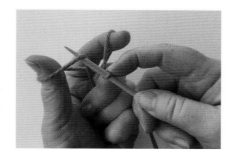 

Hold the yarn in your left hand over the
thumb and index finger with the yarn
tail to the left and the working yarn to
the right. Insert the needle down over the
yarn and out towards the left.

Insert the needle from below and up into
the thumb loop, catch the index-finger
strand from above with the needle, and
bring the yarn down through the loop on
the thumb.

Release the loop from the thumb and
pull the yarn to tighten. There are now 2
stitches on the needle. If this beginning
method is used, end the first row by knitting into the back of the last stitch.

CAST-ONS

We can't say with any certainty how the stitches were cast on traditional night sweaters. What we can see is the slant of the cast-on loops. Most point up towards the right, like this: ///.

LONG-TAIL CAST-ON ///

This method uses one needle. Calculate how much yarn will be needed for the cast-on and measure the same amount for the length of the yarn end.

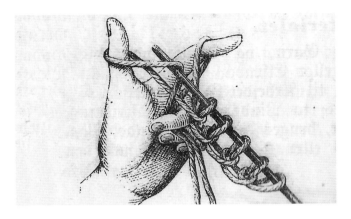

*Hold the yarn in the left hand with a long yarn end around the thumb and the working yarn around the index finger.
Hold the right needle's stitch(es) with the index finger.
Insert the needle from below and then up into the thumb loop, catch the yarn on the index finger from above and bring it down through the thumb loop. Release the loop on the thumb and bring the yarn end through*.
There is now 1 more stitch on the needle.

Repeat * to * until you have the desired number of stitches.

LOOP CAST-ON ///

This method uses one needle. The first row on this method is quite troublesome, but on the other hand you can control the stitch count along the way. Begin with the end of the yarn. You don't need to calculate a yarn amount.

Hold the needle with the beginning stitch(es) in your left hand and wrap the working yarn around the needle clockwise.
Knit 1 knit in each "wrap."
TIP: You can also wrap counterclockwise but then you should knit each stitch through the back loop on the first row.

The loop cast-on after 1 row of knitting.

KNITTED CAST-ON (K-CO) \\\

This method takes two needles. Begin with the end of the yarn. You don't need to calculate a yarn amount.

Hold the needle with the beginning stitch(es) in your left hand and the free needle in your right hand. *Knit the previous stitch, but leave the previous stitch on the left needle.

Slightly elongate the new stitch, and place it in a twisted position over the left-hand needle. There is now one more stitch on the needle. Leave the right needle in the stitch and tighten yarn*.

Repeat * to * until you have the desired number of stitches.

GERMAN TWISTED OR OLD NORWEGIAN CAST-ON ///

This method uses one needle. Calculate how much yarn will be needed for the cast-on and measure the same amount for the length of the yarn end.

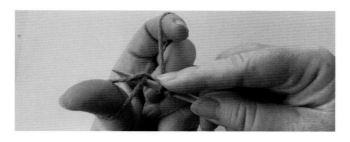

*Hold the needle as for the long-tail cast-on. Insert the needle below the entire thumb loop.

Bring the needle up and then down into the thumb loop, at the same time, forming an eyelet on the thumb so the loop's back-most strand comes through.

Now shift the needle up around the front strand on the index finger loop and bring the yarn down through the thumb eyelet loop. Release the loop and tighten yarn ends*.

Repeat * to * until you have the desired number of stitches.

THUMB LOOP CAST-ON METHOD ///

This method uses one needle. Begin with the end of the yarn. You don't need to calculate a yarn amount.

*Hold the needle with the beginning stitch(es) in your right hand and hold the working yarn with the left hand.
Insert left thumb under the yarn towards the back so it forms a loop. Twist loop as you place it on the right needle*.

Repeat * to * until you have the desired number of stitches.

INDEX FINGER LOOP CAST-ON METHOD \\\

This method uses one needle. Begin with the yarn end. You don't need to calculate a yarn amount.

Hold the needle with the beginning stitch(es) in your right hand, and hold the working yarn with your left hand. Insert your left index finger front to back below the yarn so that it makes a loop with the yarn end at the top. Twist loop as you place it on the right needle.

Repeat * to * until you have the desired number of stitches.

INCREASING

BACKWARDS LOOP INCREASE (M1-LOOP OR E-LOOP)

This increase can be worked on the RS as well as the WS.

Insert the left index finger from front to back, below the yarn strand; twist the yarn to form a loop that looks like a small letter e. Place the loop on the right needle so it forms an extra stitch exactly as described for the loop cast-on. Tighten the loop a little before you knit the next stitch.

WHICH CAST-ON?

On both Falster and Lolland, I have met with older knitters who learned how to cast on from their grandmothers. They cast on with the German twisted method /// and it looks like the same method used for most night sweaters. You can't tell the difference between the German twisted cast-on or the thumb loop cast-on and the following first knit row.

The long-tail cast-on was also used, and the possibilities are confusing when you can't tell whether the cast-on is the long-tail or clockwise loop with the following first knit row.

On some sweaters, the knitted cast-on might have been used.

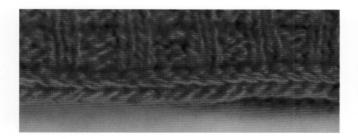

German twisted cast-on /// and a braid row knit under \\\, knitted back and forth.

German twisted cast-on /// and a braid row knit over /// knitted back and forth.

BRAID ROWS

On about 30 of the night sweaters I saw, the first row or round after the cast-on is a braid row to reinforce the cast-on row. On some of the sweaters, braid rows are also worked as decoration over the bottom edges of the body and sleeves and sometimes also before and after a horizontal panel.

TWO-END (TWINED) KNITTING

A braid row is a technique used in two-end knitting. You work with two strands, alternating the two yarns, twisting the yarns after each stitch to form a small horizontal band on the right side. If you are familiar with two-end knitting, you can use what you have learned. Both strands are held in the right hand with this technique.

CHART SYMBOLS

I've seen four different braids on the original night sweaters. All of the braids are indicated with the same symbol on the book's charts. The written instructions will indicate which of the four braid methods to use.

YARN FOR BRAIDS

When working a braid in one color, it's a good idea to use yarn from both the inside and outside of the yarn ball. As the yarn becomes twisted, you can 'lock" the outside yarn with a short needle, release the ball so it turns freely, and turn the ball to untwist the strands. If you're going to work only one braid row, you can calculate how much yarn you need for the cast-on plus the braid row and simply use the yarn tail for both rows.

The following pages describe how to work braids with the yarn held in the left hand, which is the usual way of knitting in Denmark. The yarn is held over the fingers as for two-color stranded knitting.

To clarify the techniques, I cast on with green yarn and then knitted with two colors (1 strand green, 1 strand orange) to make it easier to see the process.

Always begin by knitting the first stitch on each row with both strands.

BRAID ROW KNIT OVER ///

Rows worked back and forth.
Worked on WS and shows on RS.

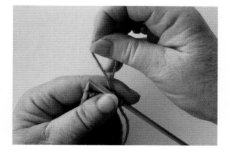

Place both strands over the index finger of left hand with the orange at the top of the finger (near the nail). Knit 1 with the orange yarn.

Twist the strands so that the front (orange) strand comes over the back (green) strand. Now position the green yarn nearest the nail. Knit 1 with green. *Twist green over orange and knit 1 orange. Cross orange over green and knit 1 green*.

Repeat * to * across.

BRAID ROW KNIT UNDER \\\

Worked back and forth.
Worked on WS and shows on RS.

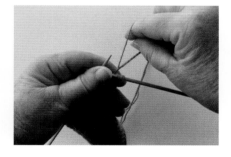

Work as for the braid knit over but twist the strands counterclockwise—that is, under rather than over after each stitch as follows:
Position both strands on the left index finger with the orange at the top of the finger (near the nail). Knit 1 with orange yarn.

Twist the strands so the front (orange) strand comes under the back (green) strand. Now position the green yarn nearest the nail. Knit 1 with green. *Twist green under orange and knit 1 orange. Cross orange under green and knit 1 green*.

Repeat * to * across.

BRAID ROW PURL OVER ///

Worked in the round or on RS of flat knitting.
Worked on RS and shows on RS.

Position both strands on the left index finger (holding both strands at the front of the work) with the orange at the top of the finger (near the nail). Insert the right needle into the stitch from below and up between both strands, purl 1 with orange yarn.

Twist the strands so that the front (orange) strand crosses over the back (green) strand. Now position the green yarn nearest the nail. *Purl 1 with green the same way the orange was purled. Twist green over orange and purl 1 orange*.

Repeat * to * around.

BRAID ROW PURL UNDER \\\

Worked in the round or on RS of flat knitting.
Worked on RS and shows on RS.

Position both strands on the left index finger (holding both strands at the front of the work) with the orange at the top of the finger (near the nail). Insert the right needle into the stitch from below and up between both strands, purl 1 with orange yarn.

Twist the strands so that the outermost (orange) strand crosses under the back (green) strand. Now position the green yarn nearest the nail. *Purl 1 with green the same way the orange was purled. Twist green under orange and purl 1 orange *.

Repeat * to * around.

TRAVELING STITCHES

Quite a few night sweaters—especially those from Falster—display some rather advanced patterns, where traveling stitches move over knit and purl lines. We don't know how people knitted these designs in the 19th century but there are several methods for doing so. Try each of the following methods and use the one you like best.

Falster sweaters were often knitted in the round with stockinette from above the bottom edge to about where the armhole begins. The piece was then divided for front and back and worked back and forth. This is where the traveling stitch patterns began. If it's too difficult to knit traveling stitches in the round, there's nothing to stop you from knitting them back and forth.

CHART SYMBOLS

The four different symbols for the traveling stitches are explained in one way for working on the right side and another way on the wrong side.

Knitting Tip: The first row is the most difficult; after that it becomes possible to see how the stitches should travel. If you compare what's on your needles with the symbols on the chart, you'll see that traveling stitches turn as for the symbol you are knitting from. When working on the wrong side, it's a good idea to tilt the work occasionally so that you can see how it looks on the right side.

NOTE: When it says "knit into the stitch from the back" on the following pages, it's to avoid a stitch becoming twisted.

RN = needle in right hand.
LN = needle in left hand.

TRAVELING STITCHES WORKED ON THE RIGHT SIDE

= CROSS 2 KNIT STS LEFT

= CROSS 2 KNIT STS RIGHT

Method 1: Twisted stitches—Vivian's method

Slip 1 st knitwise, slip 1 more st knitwise, insert LN through RN's second and first sts in that order towards the left. Slip both sts, together at same time, back to the LN. The sts are now crossed. Knit each of the two sts.

Method 2: Pass stitches over

Knit the LN's second st behind the first st through back loop and leave the sts on the LN. Now knit the first st and let both sts drop from the needle.

Method 3: Using a cable needle

Place the first st on a cable needle and hold in front of the work, knit 1, and then knit the st on cable needle.

Method 1: Twisted stitches—Vivian's method

Slip 2 sts knitwise at the same time and then place them together back on LN. The stitches are now crossed. Knit each of the 2 sts through back loops.

Method 2: Pass stitches over

Knit the second st on LN in front of the first and leave sts on LN. Knit the first st and drop both sts from the needle.

Method 3: Using a cable needle

Place the first st on a cable needle and hold behind the work, knit 1, and then knit the st on cable needle.

⊞ = CROSS 1 PURL AND 1 KNIT ST LEFT

⊞ = CROSS 1 KNIT AND 1 PURL RIGHT

Method 1: Twisted stitches—Vivian's method

Slip 1 knitwise and then slip 1 more st knitwise. Insert LN through the RN's 2nd st and then first st towards the left; slip the 2 sts together, at the same time, back onto LN. The stitches are now crossed. Purl 1, knit 1.

Method 2: Pass stitches over

Purl second st on LN from behind the first st (twisting st if that is easier) and leave sts on LN. Knit the first st and then drop both sts from needle.

Method 3: Using a cable needle

Place the first st on a cable needle and hold in front of the work, purl 1, and then knit st on cable needle.

Method 1: Twisted stitches—Vivian's method

Slip 2 sts together knitwise at the same time and then slide them back to LN. The stitches are now crossed. Knit 1, purl 1, both through back loop.

Method 2: Pass stitches over

Knit second st on LN in front of the first st and leave sts on LN. Purl the first st and then drop both sts from needle.

Method 3: Using a cable needle

Place the first st on a cable needle and hold in back of the work, knit 1, and then purl st on cable needle.

TRAVELING STITCHES WORKED ON THE WRONG SIDE

= CROSS 2 PURL STS TO THE LEFT

= CROSS 2 PURL STS TO THE RIGHT

Method 1: Twisted stitches—Vivian's method

Slip 1 st knitwise, slip 1 more st knitwise, insert LN through RN's second and first sts in that order towards the left. Slip both sts together back to the LN at the same time. The sts are now crossed. Purl each of the two sts.

Method 1: Twisted stitches—Vivian's method

Slip 2 sts knitwise at the same time and then slip them together back on LN. The stitches are now crossed. Purl each of the 2 sts through back loops.

Method 2: Pass stitches over

Purl the LN's second st from behind the first st through back loop and leave the sts on the LN. Now purl the first st and let both sts drop from the needle.

Method 2: Pass stitches over

Purl the second st on LN in front of the first and leave sts on LN. Purl the first st and drop both sts from the needle.

Method 3: Using a cable needle

Place the first st on a cable needle and hold in front of the work, purl 1, and then knit the st on cable needle.

Method 3: Using a cable needle

Place the first st on a cable needle and hold behind the work, purl 1, and then purl the st on cable needle.

**▣ = CROSS 1 PURL AND
1 KNIT TOWARDS THE LEFT**

**▣ = CROSS 1 KNIT AND
1 PURL TOWARDS THE RIGHT**

Method 1: Twisted stitches—Vivian's method

Slip 1 knitwise and then slip the next st knitwise. Insert the LN through RN's second st and then first st, towards the left, and slip the 2 sts together onto LN at same time. The stitches are now crossed. Purl 1, knit 1.

Method 2: Pass stitches over

Purl second st on LN from behind the first st in back loop and leave sts on LN. Knit the first st and then drop both sts from needle.

Method 3: Using a cable needle.

Place the first st on a cable needle and hold in front of the work, purl 1, and then knit the st on cable needle.

Method 1: Twisted stitches—Vivian's method

Slip 2 sts together knitwise at the same time and then slip them back to LN. The stitches are now crossed. Knit 1, purl 1 each through back loops.

Method 2: Pass stitches over

Knit second st on LN in front of the first st and leave sts on LN. Purl the first st and then drop both sts from needle.

Method 3: Using a cable needle

Place the first st on a cable needle and hold in back of the work, knit 1, and then purl the st on cable needle.

HORIZONTAL STITCHES

These stitches are similar to traveling stitches but are a bit different to knit. Stars with a knitted horizontal band appear on only one sweater from North Ørslev (LFS 7007, page 29). The row with the horizontal stitches needs to be knitted firmly.

Begin by increasing 1 stitch (with kf&b = knit into front and then back of same stitch).
Slip the first st on right needle to left needle, knit the second stitch on left needle from behind the first stitch, and leave the sts on the needle; knit the first stitch (the horizontal one).
Repeat * to *.
End by moving the horizontal stitch to the left needle and knitting it together with the next stitch.

Alternatively, you can purl the second stitch and then knit the first stitch, but this method is not used in this book.

HORIZONTAL STITCHES BEHIND VERTICAL STITCHES

A horizontal stitch can be worked behind a vertical stockinette stitch as follows:

Place the vertical stitch on a cable needle and hold in front of work, move the first st on the right needle to the left needle, place the stitch on the cable needle back on the left needle, and knit it.

Now continue working horizontal stitches as before.

CHART SYMBOLS

Three symbols are used in connection with horizontal stitches: one symbol is for the initial 2-in-1 stitch, one for the concluding k2tog, and the third for the horizontal stitches in between.

In the center of the star shown here, 1 horizontal stitch is behind 1 vertical stitch. On the chart, this is shown by a fourth symbol (see pattern S-28 on page 87).

Star S-28

OVERLAPPING EDGES

Several of the Falster sweaters are joined at the sides of the lower edges, in which the outermost stitches from the respective back and front pieces overlap as for a cabled cord. Besides being decorative, the overlapped cords reinforce the join. Very many sweaters are simply joined without any form of reinforcement and they are just as often torn at the join.

THREE-NEEDLE BIND-OFF

This method for finishing is used on most of the night sweaters for joining shoulders rather than a sewn seam and so it is also used in this book. You will need 3 double-pointed needles: 2 to hold the stitches for each of the pieces to be joined and 1 more to knit with.

Turn the work so the WS faces out. Place the stitches of the front right shoulder on a needle and the stitches of the back right shoulder on another needle.

Hold the two needles parallel and knit the first stitch on each needle together, *knit the next stitch on each needle together, pass the back stitch on the right needle over the previous one*.

Repeat * to * until only 1 stitch remains. Make sure that the join is not too tight as you work. Cut yarn and bring end through last loop.

Join the left shoulder the same way.

PATTERN MOTIFS

200 PATTERN MOTIFS

Danish night sweaters from the 19th century contain a world of patterns. On first glance at a sweater, the patterns might seem almost insignificant and minimalist, but a closer inspection will reveal fabric with one interesting detail after another. The abundant richness of patterning they have to share is completely unique.

At any rate, they've scarcely been described, charted, or used since they were part of Danish day-to-day dress. The single-color sweaters at museums are often so felted that the patterns are only hinted at, which is why I've had to guess sometimes. I've stayed as true to the originals as possible.

TYPES OF PATTERNS
All the designs were charted and then sample-knitted. The charts and test samples are shown on the following pages. I divided the patterns into six groups, according to where they're placed on the sweaters.

stars—alone or within a main pattern;
horizontal panels—often above the lower edge or at the shoulders;
vertical traveling stitch and star motifs—along the neck/armholes;
vertical panels—often along the side seams and sometimes all the way down to the edge;
main pattern—the pattern covering the body or sleeves;
edge patterns—lower edge of the body and sleeves.

KNITTING TECHNIQUES
Very few techniques were actually used; the motifs are mostly simple and easy to knit, with only knit and purl stitches. Some sweaters were rather more sophisticated and decorated with twisted and crossed stitches. Common to all is exclusive embellishment on the surface and the use of only one color of yarn.

Traveling stitches were in style, especially on Falster, even when the pieces were knitted back and forth (which is rather difficult). In this case, twisted knit stitches were used quite often on older sweaters. Certain motifs, such as stars, have a twisted knit stitch at the center but only regular knit stitches in other areas.

On some of my test swatches, I decided to work a regular knit stitch instead of a twisted knit stitch when the pattern is symmetrical, regardless of how it was worked on the original sweater, because I think it looks nicest. On the charts, a twisted knit is always shown in a yellow square, to make it easy to see.

FOR INSPIRATION
These pattern motifs can be used in all their simplicity, any way you like—over entire surfaces, or in smaller areas. On pages 232-241, you'll find advice for how to design your own sweater using these motifs.

Be inspired!

FIND A MOTIF

When a motif is used in one of the garments with instructions on pages 140-231, it will be referred to by number as follows. The first letter refers to the pattern type.

S-1 to S-41: Stars
H-1 to H-14: Horizontal panels.
VT-1 to VT-9: Vertical traveling stitch and star motifs
V-1 to V-64: Vertical panels
M-1 to M-39: Main patterns
E-1 to E-37: Edge patterns

INFORMATION ABOUT THE INDIVIDUAL PATTERNS

Place =	The name of the town/place from which a sweater was obtained, or where it had been worn.
Repeat =	The number of stitches and rows/rounds to be repeated across the width and/or in length whether the pattern is used in a panel or across the surface. The repeat is blocked off on the chart within a red frame.
Multiple of =	The number of stitches within a pattern repeat.
… plus =	The number of stitches to be added to a repeat so that a pattern will be symmetrical and will begin and end the same way. In this book, this applies to horizontal panels and edges.
RS and WS =	Particular edge stitches can be used on both the right side (RS) and wrong side (WS).

STARS

There are stars on 54 of the 87 sweaters I examined, for a total of 34 distinct star designs. One of the sweaters (LFS 7007) even sports 5 different stars (the North Ørslev sweater on page 29). It wouldn't be wrong to say that stars are the most popular motifs for night sweaters. Most of them are presented on the following pages.

CLASSIC STARS

The star most often seen is the absolutely classic simple star with 8 points, knitted in reverse stockinette against a stockinette background and divided by a vertical stockinette or twisted stitch. See, for example, S-1. In general, stars are worked in several sizes on each sweater.

OTHER STARS

Among the many star variations is one with seed stitch diagonal lines (S-9), where two tips (one on each side) point downwards, so the star has what I think of as a wistful expression. This pattern can be found consistently worked over a whole sweater, so we know for sure it wasn't error. There are stars with a purl diamond at the center (S-13) or with 4 seed stitch and 4 purl stitch points (S-11), as on the sweater from Moseby on Falster (LFS 16285) to the right. There are stars with ingenious traveling stitches (S-20 through S-38); many are exquisite with their harmonious designs, such as S-24 from the Seattle sweater (page 23). Finally, some of the sweaters show unusual techniques, as in S-27 and S-28, with a horizontal stockinette stitch (see page 76). I have previously only seen this technique used in Estonia.

TALL STARS

Some of the sweaters have tall, elongated stars. One of these is a sweater from Aastrup on Falster with lovely, tall stars within a netting of traveling stitches centered on the sleeves—for examples, see S-37 and S-38. The stars on the Eskilstrup sweater (pattern instructions on page

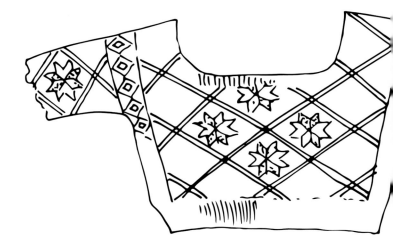

150) are also tall, and worked in reverse stockinette and vertical twisted stitches. Finally, the Lolland sweater LFS 23885a (page 47) has very harmonic, perfectly squared stars which, on closer examination, have more rows than stitches (see S-17 and S-18). In stockinette/damask knitting, a square consists of more rows than stitches, which is the reason why most of the stars are actually wider than they are high.

STAR SYMBOLISM

Stars are an entire world to themselves. They're lovely shapes, and in the context of handworked motifs, they're simple and easy to construct. Stars are Christian symbols, of course; a star led the three wise men from the East to the stable where they found Mary and Jesus. But the use of star symbols here also has an element of superstition and serves to provide protection. Night sweaters fitted tightly on the body and were worn day and night, so it must have seemed only natural to knit in protective symbols. I've also been told that the stars are holes in the night sky which lead directly to Heaven. What could be better?

S-1, 33 sts x 33 rows/rnds.

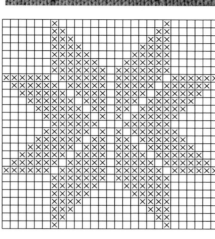

S-2, 27 sts x 27 rows/rnds.

S-3, 25 sts x 29 rows/rnds.

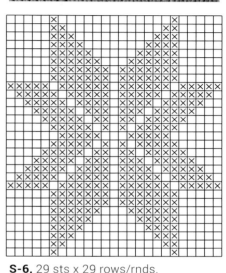

S-4, 23 sts x 21 rows/rnds.

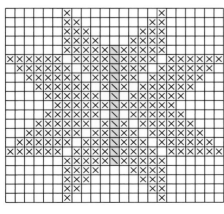

S-5, 27 sts x 29 rows/rnds.

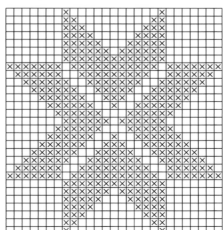

S-6, 29 sts x 29 rows/rnds.

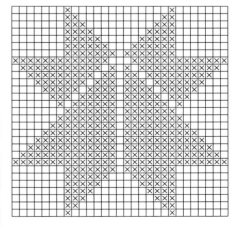

S-7, 29 sts x 29 rows/rnds.

S-8, 21 sts x 21 rows/rnds.

S-9, 33 sts x 33 rows/rnds.

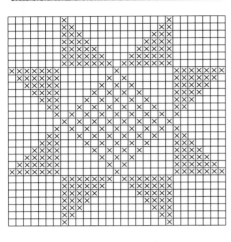

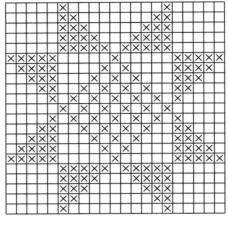

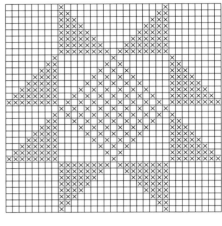

S-10, 33 sts x 33 rows/rnds.

S-11, 25 sts x 27 rows/rnds.

S-12, 17 sts x 17 rows/rnds.

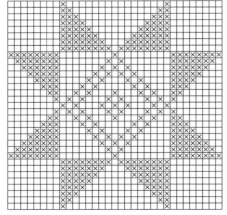

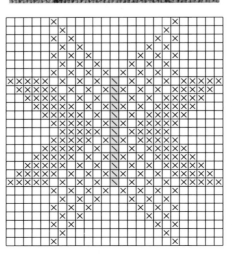

S-13, 25 sts x 25 rows/rnds.

S-14, 19 sts x 12 rows/rnds.

S-15, 23 sts x 17 rows/rnds.

S-16, 21 sts x 21 rows/rnds.

S-17, 25 sts x 29 rows/rnds.

S-18, 27 sts x 31 rows/rnds.

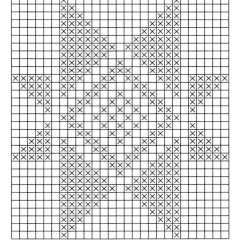
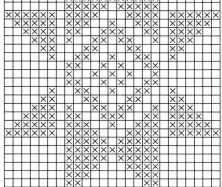

PATTERN MOTIFS

S-19, 33 sts x 33 rows/rnds.

S-20, 26 sts x 25 rows/rnds.

S-21, 26 sts x 27 rows/rnds.

S-22, 28 sts x 27 rows/rnds.

S-23, 23 sts x 21 rows/rnds.

S-24, 26 sts x 25 rows/rnds.

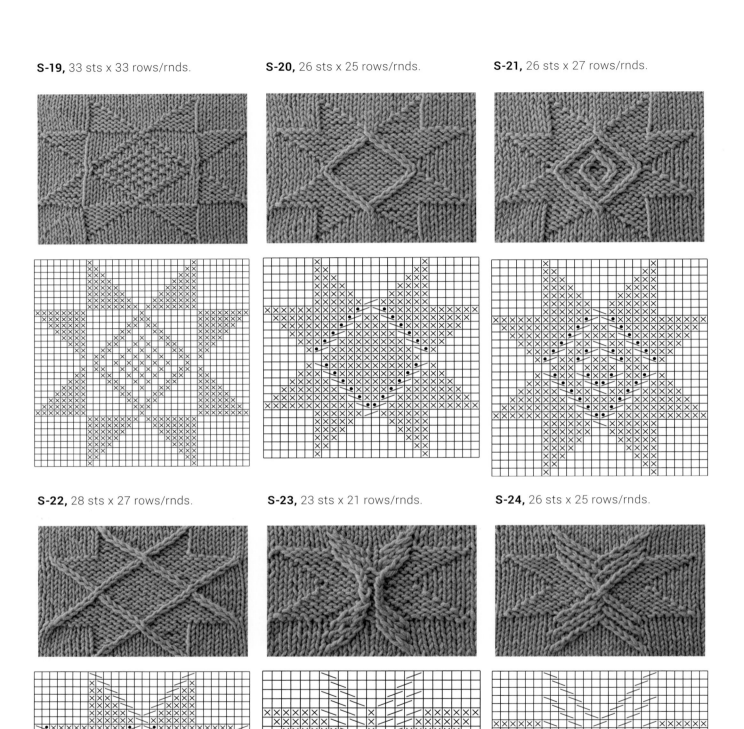

S-25, 26 sts x 25 rows/rnds.

S-26, 24 sts x 26 rows/rnds.

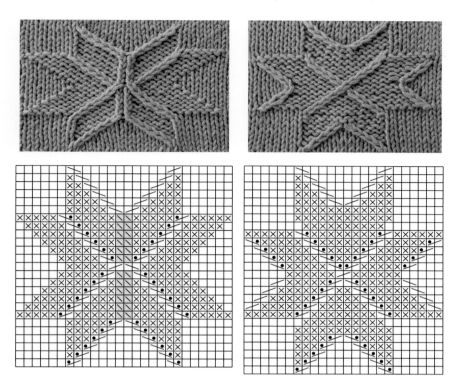

S-27, 25 sts x 25 rows/rnds.

S-28, 27 sts x 27 rows/rnds.

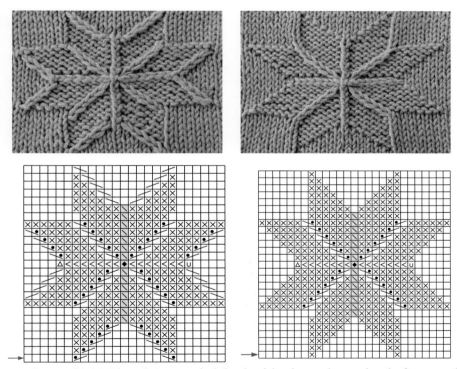

On S-27 and S-28: The red arrow at the left side of the chart indicates that the first row of the star is worked on the WS so the center horizontal band can be worked on the RS.

S-29, 18 sts x 19 rows/rnds.

S-30, 19 sts x 19 rows/rnds.

S-31, 27 sts x 24 rows/rnds.

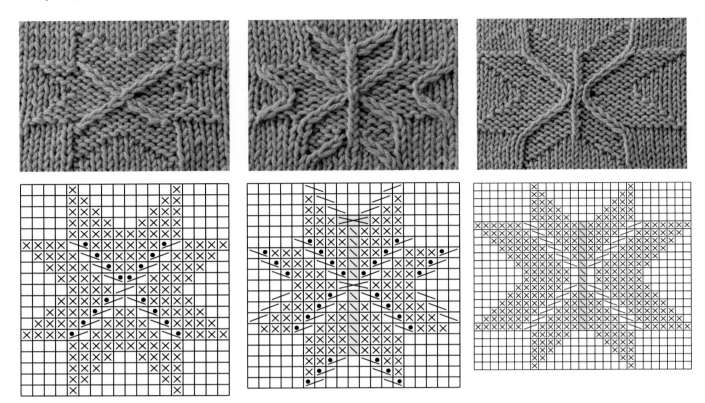

S-32, 38 sts x 39 rows/rnds.

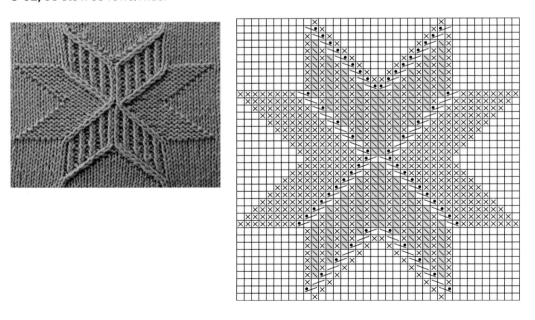

S-33, 39 sts x 39 rows/rnds.

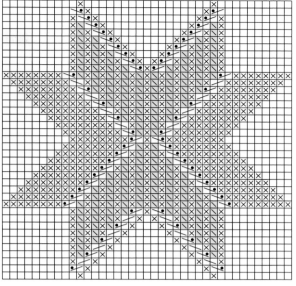

S-34, 26 sts x 27 rows/rnds.

S-35, 28 sts x 29 rows/rnds.

S-36, 30 sts x 30 rows/rnds.

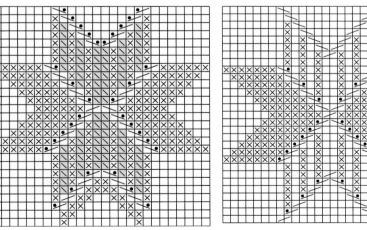

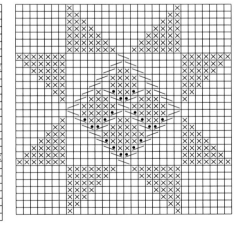

S-37, 22 sts x 31 rows/rnds.　　　**S-38,** 24 sts x 37 rows/rnds.

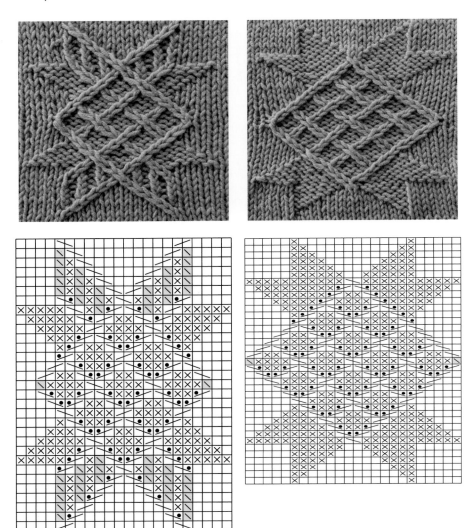

S-39, 27 sts x 43 rows/rnds.

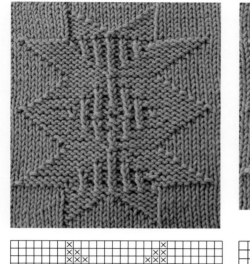

S-40, 23 sts x 37 rows/rnds.

S-41, 25 sts x 39 rows/rnds.

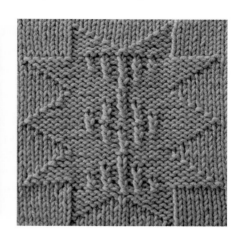

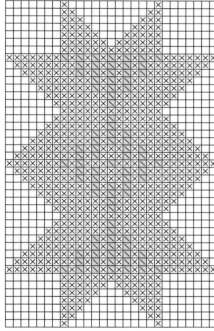

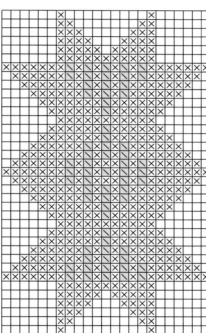

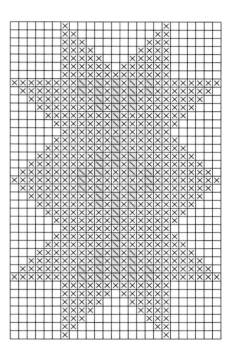

HORIZONTAL PANELS

Night sweaters from Lolland often have a horizontal panel above the lower edges on the body or sleeves, and sometimes along the shoulder seams, as on this sweater from West Ulslev on Lolland (LFS 16080). However, some of the panels have been hidden behind sewn-on silk ribbons.

The panels are simple, often zig-zag patterns that can be used in many ways and are easy to vary. They can, for example, be copied and inverted to transform a zigzag panel into a diamond (see H-4, for example).

The seed stitch panels—for example, H-2—can be further embellished with small glass beads, if you like.

REPEATS
The stitches and rows/rounds surrounded by a red frame are repeated to the left. If you want symmetrical panels on each side, generally you'll need to add a stitch, which will be indicated with "+" 1 (= plus 1 stitch).

H-1
Multiple of 10 sts + 1.
Height: 7 rows/rnds.

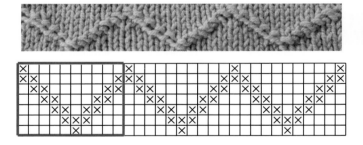

H-2
Multiple of 12 sts + 1.
Height: 12 rows/rnds.

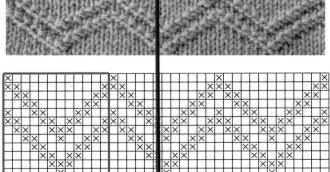

H-3

Multiple of 20 sts.
Height: 11 rows/rnds.

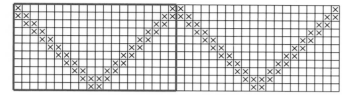

H-4

Multiple of 12 sts + 1.
Height: 15 rows/rnds.

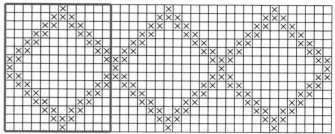

H-5

Multiple of 12 sts + 1.
Height: 11 rows/rnds.

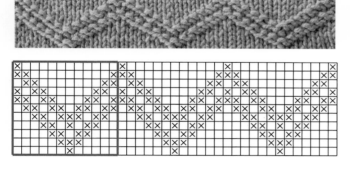

H-6

Multiple of 16 sts + 1.
Height: 13 rows/rnds.

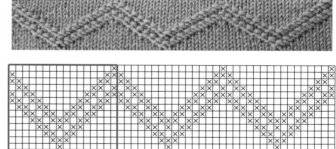

H-7

Multiple of 10 sts + 1.
Height: 8 rows/rnds.

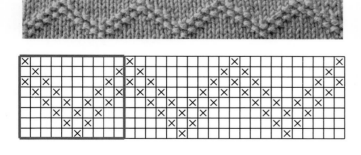

H-8

Multiple of 12 sts + 1.
Height: 11 rows/rnds.

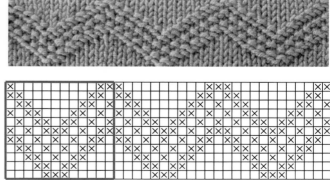

H-9

Multiple of 12 sts + 1.
Height: 25 rows/rnds.

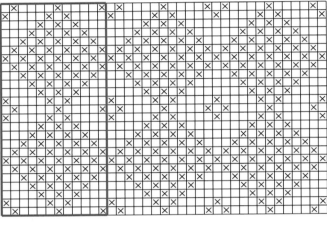

H-10

Multiple of 16 sts + 1.
Height: 17 rows/rnds.

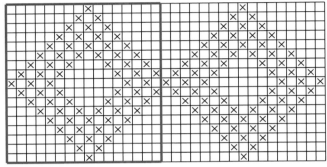

H-11

Multiple of 10 sts.
Height: 19 rows/rnds.

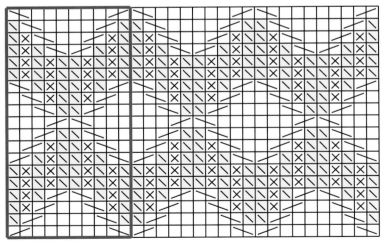

H-12

Multiple of 12 sts + 1.
Height: 30 rows/rnds.

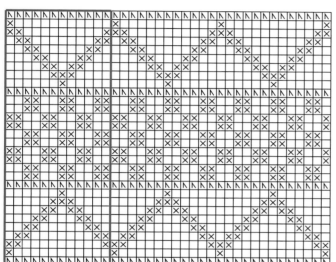

H-13

Multiple of 26 sts + 1.
Height: 37 rows/rnds.

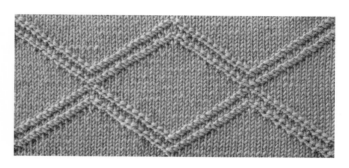

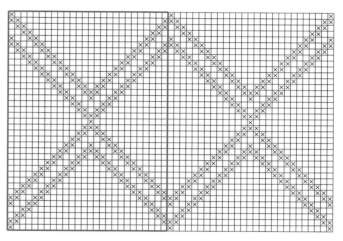

H-14

Multiple of 12 sts + 1.
Height: 29 rows/rnds.

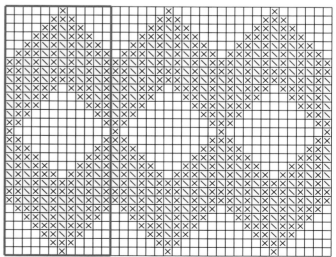

VERTICAL TRAVELING STITCH AND STAR MOTIFS

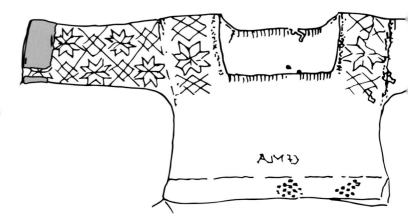

This category of patterns includes wide, vertical panels, which run up both the front and back to meet at the "shoulder seam," which most often is positioned on the front and not at the shoulder.

The panels typically consist of alternating traveling stitches and a star, as can be seen on this sweater from Odense (KMO/1963/613, page 53); other times there are only traveling stitches.

On certain Falster sweaters, a vertical traveling stitch and star motif is knitted up to the shoulders between the armhole and the front neck. These patterns are flanked by vertical panels.

REPEATS
The stitches and rows/rounds surrounded by a red frame can be repeated in length.

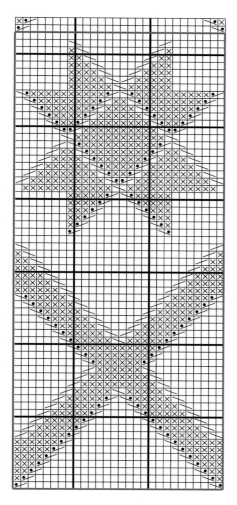

VT-1
Place: North Kirkeby, Falster.
Repeat: 28 sts x 63 rows/rnds.

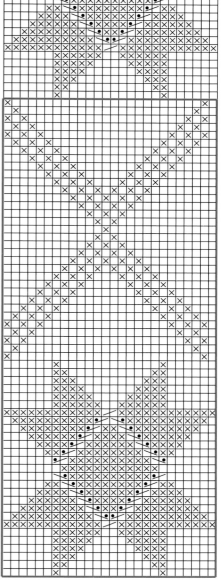

VT-2
Place: Sullerup, Falster.
Repeat: 26 sts x 60 rows/rnds.

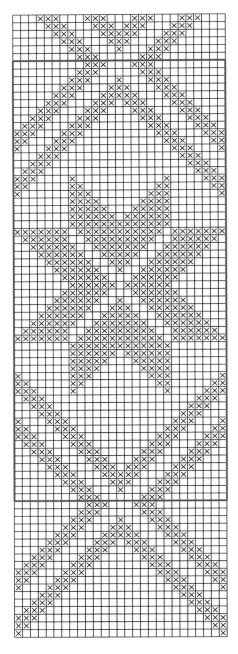

VT-3
Place: Aastrup, Falster.
Repeat: 27 sts x 58 rows/rnds.

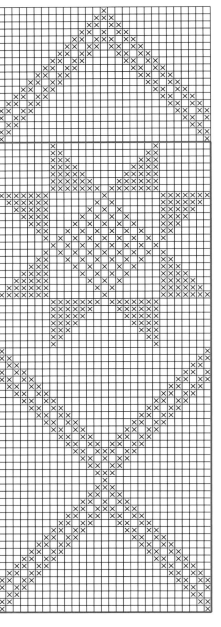

VT-4
Place: North Alstrup, Falster.
Owned by Helene Strange.
Repeat: 29 sts x 66 rows/rnds.

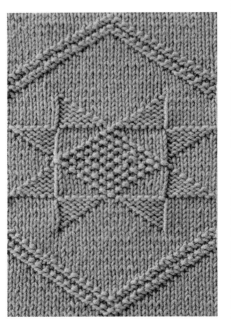

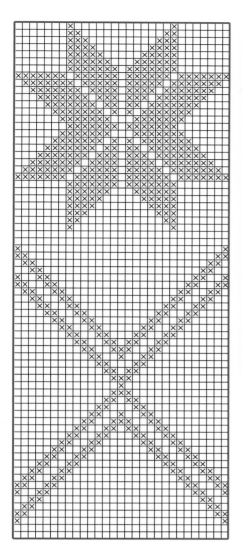

VT-5

Place: Unknown.

Repeat: 29 sts x 72 rows/rnds.

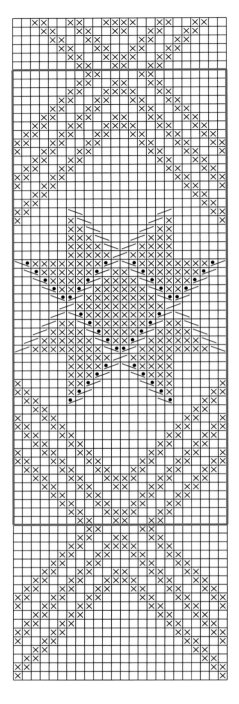

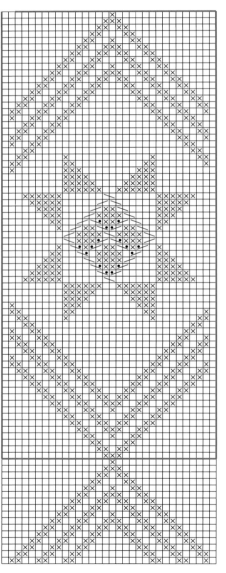

VT-7
Place: Karleby, Falster.
Repeat: 32 sts x 69 rows/rnds.

VT-8

Place: Stubbekøbing, Falster.

Repeat: 55 sts x 58 rows/rnds.

VT-9

Place: Vejringe, Falster.

Repeat: 39 sts x 24 rows/rnds.

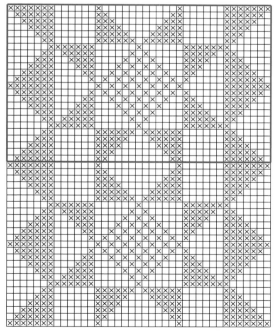

VERTICAL PANELS

Vertical panels often flanked the vertical traveling stitch and star motifs on the body and, in many instances, along the armholes. Sometimes these panels extended all the way down to the lower edge as a sort of side seam or perhaps just as a narrow panel to separate the gusset from the back/front pieces.

Quite a few of the patterns were worked with only knit and purl stitches, while others had more complex traveling stitch patterns, such as V-45 and V-46. Some of the sweaters featured several vertical panels side by side. The sweater from North Ørslev (LFS 7007, page 29) is an absolute masterpiece. Still others repeated the vertical panels up to the underarms, as on the sweater to the right from South Aslev (FMN 1025a).

NOTE: When the twisted knit or traveling stitches are symmetrically arranged (V-59, for instance), I have chosen to work the knits as regular knits and not twisted—even if the stitches are twisted on the original sweater.

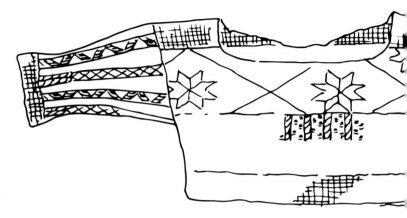

REPEATS

The stitches and rows/rounds surrounded by a red frame can be repeated in height. If you want to repeat them across the width, usually you'll need to add one or more stitches between the vertical panels to separate them.

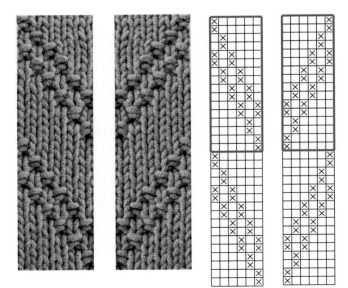

V-1 and V-2
Repeat: 6 sts x 16 rows/rnds.

V-3 and V-4
Repeat: 6 sts x 16 rows/rnds.

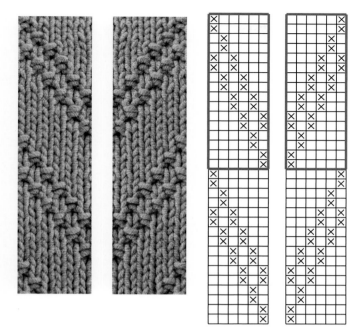

V-5
Repeat: 7 sts x 12 rows/rnds.

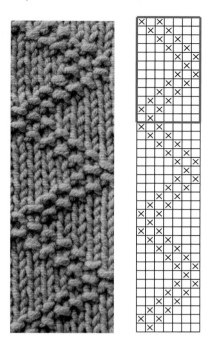

V-6 and V-7
Repeat: 10 sts x 14 rows/rnds.

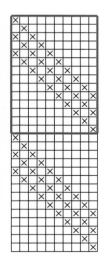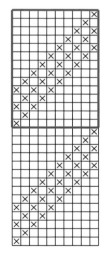

V-8
Repeat: 13 sts x 7 rows/rnds.

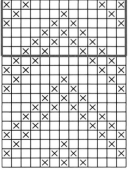

V-9
Repeat: 35 sts x 30 rows/rnds.

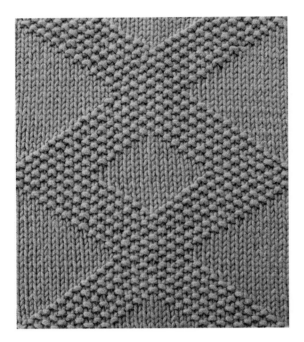
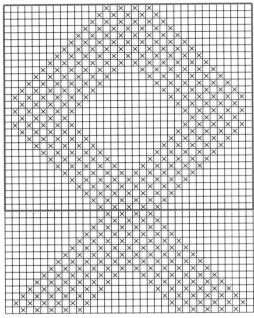

V-10
Repeat: 15 sts x 30 rows/rnds.

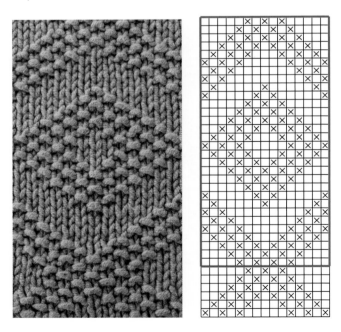

V-11
Repeat: 17 sts x 16 rows/rnds.

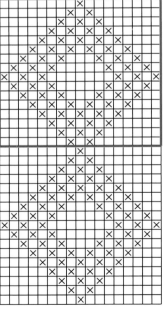

V-12

Repeat: 19 sts x 13 rows/rnds.

V-13 and V-14

Repeat: 7 sts x 14 rows/rnds.

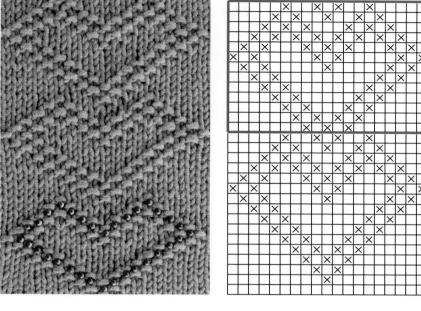

V-15 and V-16

Repeat: 10 sts x 4 rows/rnds.

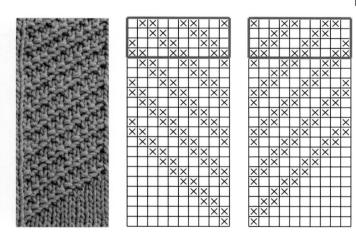

V-17

Repeat: 26 sts x 4 rows/rnds.

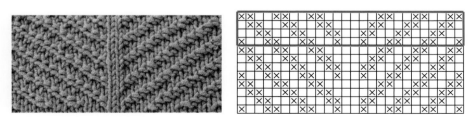

V-18 and V-19
Repeat: 7 sts x 8 rows/rnds.

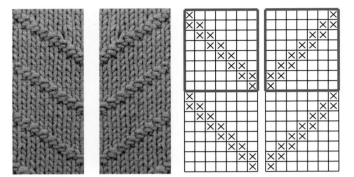

V-20 and V-21
Repeat: 8 sts x 7 rows/rnds.

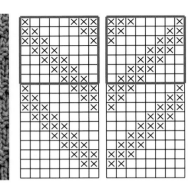

V-22
Repeat: 6 sts x 8 rows/rnds.

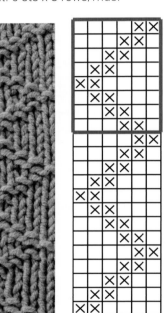

V-23
Repeat: 9 sts x 14 rows/rnds.

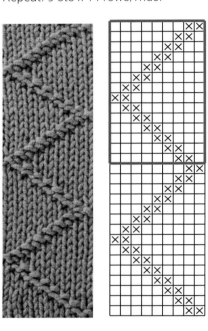

V-24
Repeat: 6 sts x 12 rows/rnds.

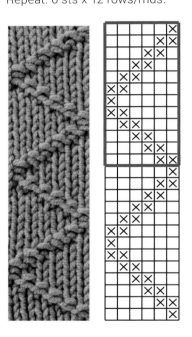

V-25

Repeat: 27 sts x 14 rows/rnds.

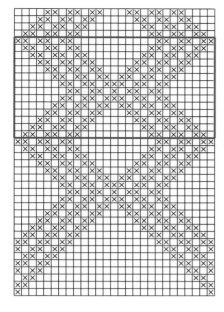

V-26

Repeat: 13 sts x 12 rows/rnds.

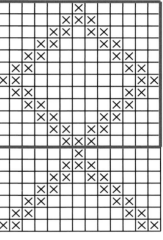

V-27

Repeat: 17 sts x 24 rows/rnds.

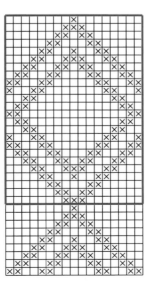

V-28

Repeat: 9 sts x 10 rows/rnds.

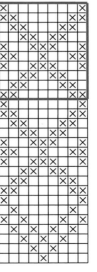

V-29
Repeat: 17 sts x 12 rows/rnds.

V-30 and V-31
Repeat: 6 sts x 10 rows/rnds.

V-32 and V-33
Repeat: 8 sts x 14 rows/rnds.

V-34 and V-35
Repeat: 13 sts x 20 rows/rnds.

V-36 and V-37
Repeat: 9 sts x 10 rows/rnds.

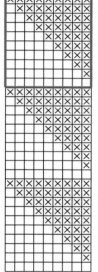 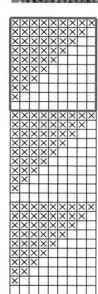

V-38
Repeat: 4 sts x 2 rows/rnds.
15 sts x 40 rows/rnds.
5 sts x 4 rows/rnds.

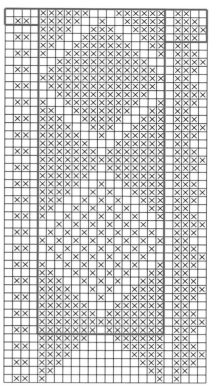

V-39
Repeat: 3 sts x 2 rows/rnds.
7 sts x 19 rows/rnds.
3 sts x 2 rows/rnds.

 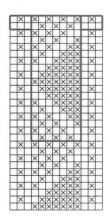

V-40
Repeat: 5 sts x 34 rows/rnds.
4 sts x 4 rows/rnds.
5 sts x 34 rows/rnds.

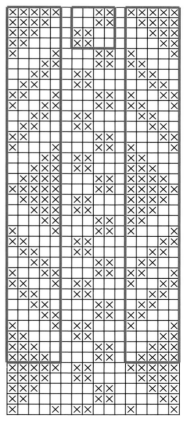

V-41
Repeat: 10 sts x 5 rows/rnds.

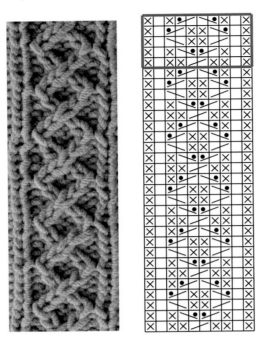

V-42
Repeat: 10 sts x 8 rows/rnds.

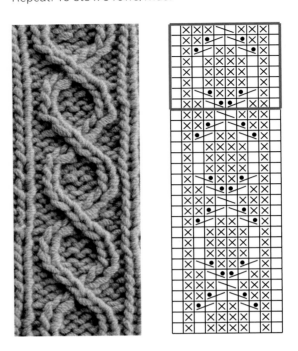

V-43
Repeat: 20 sts x 19 rows/rnds.

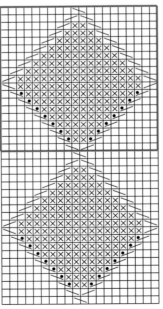

V-44
Repeat: 12 sts x 7 rows/rnds.

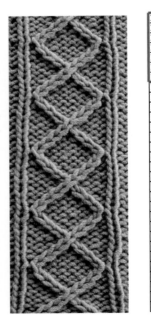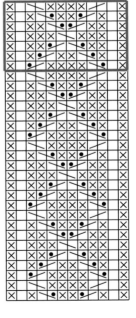

V-45

Repeat: 2 sts x 4 rows/rnds.
12 sts x 6 rows/rnds.
2 sts x 4 rows/rnds.

V-46

Repeat: 18 sts x 6 rows/rnds.

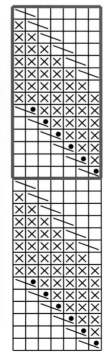

V-47 and V-48

Repeat: 7 sts x 12 rows/rnds.

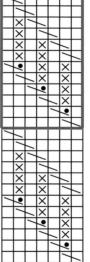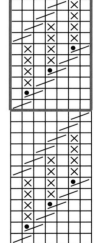

V-49 and V-50

Repeat: 7 sts x 14 rows/rnds.

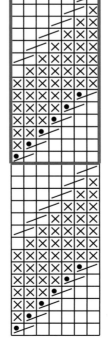

V-51
Repeat: 8 sts x 12 rows/rnds.

V-52
Repeat: 7 sts x 14 rows/rnds.

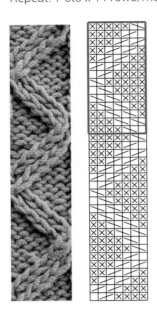

V-53
Repeat: 7 sts x 22 rows/rnds.

V-54
Repeat: 13 sts x 42 rows/rnds.

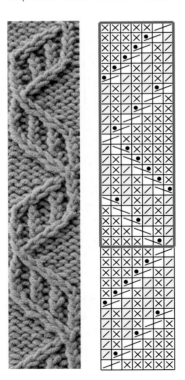

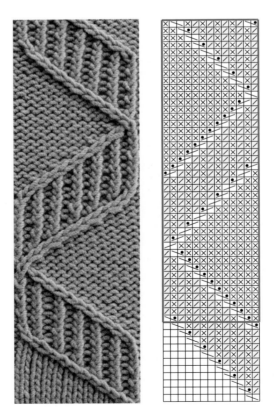

V-55
Repeat: 12 sts x 18 rows/rnds.

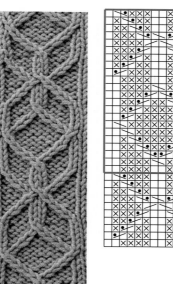

V-56
Repeat: 14 sts x 22 rows/rnds.

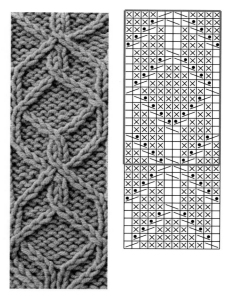

V-57
Repeat: 12 sts x 20 rows/rnds.

V-58
Repeat: 16 sts x 20 rows/rnds.

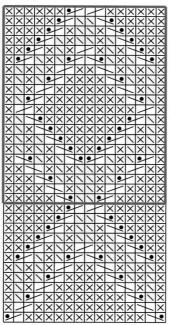

V-59
Repeat: 12 sts x 12 rows/rnds.

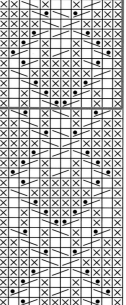

V-60

Repeat: 34 sts x 20 rows/rnds.

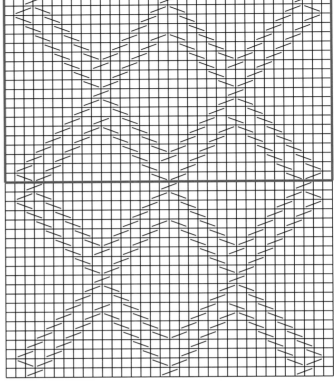

V-61

Repeat: 28 sts x 11 rows/rnds.

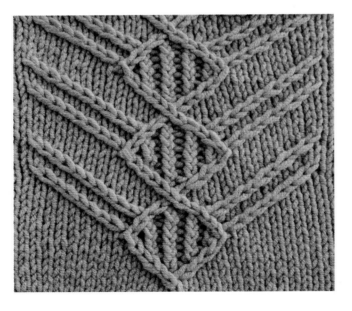

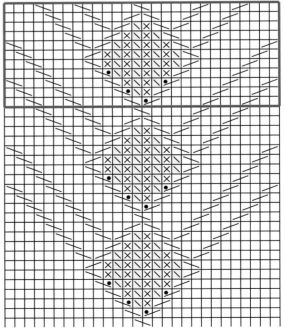

V-62

Repeat: 5 sts x 4 rows/rnds.

V-63

Repeat: 6 sts x 2 rows/rnds.

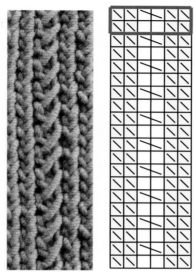

V-64

Repeat: 3 sts x 2 rows/rnds.

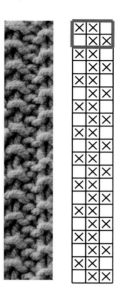

MAIN PATTERNS

A main pattern is, as the phrase suggests, an overall design. These patterns usually consist of a diagonal netting of traveling stitch lines, often surrounding knitted stars.

TRAVELING STITCH AND STAR MOTIFS

Patterns with a diamond-shaped netting of traveling stitches combined with stars appear on both the body and sleeves of garments from around the country—as well as on the oldest knitted silk night shirts. One example is this sweater from Herning (20960, pages 26 and 27).

Beloved children have many names, as we say in Denmark, and it's no different with this type of pattern. It is called a *drejlsstrikning* ("drill knitting"—likely named after drill weave, with its distinctive diagonal pattern lines) pattern in the Holbæk region, *bunden* (also, *bundet* or *strikket*) *i stjerner* (knitted in stars) in Sorø; in the Hedebo region, these patterns are known as *gramaser*, and on Drejø, they are called *krammønstre* (small patterns). In this book, we refer to them as traveling stitch and star patterns.

TRAVELING STITCHES

On many sweaters, the stars are omitted so the traveling stitches form the netting. I call these patterns traveling stitch designs. The traveling stitches are formed by single, double, or triple stitch lines with 1, 2, or 3 purl stitches or with seed stitch lines. Often the holes or diamonds between the traveling stitches are larger on the body than on the sleeves.

INCREASING WITHIN THE PATTERN

On the sleeves, traveling stitch and star patterns are formed such that the increases can be incorporated into the pattern. Both traveling stitches and stars are simply enlarged by the increases as they go up the sleeves. Increases

were not added as we do now, up the underarm seam on every 4th or 6th row/round. No, two stitches are increased per traveling stitch line and two stitches per star and, correspondingly, an extra pair of rows are automatically added for each pattern repeat. It's complicated to describe this in a pattern and even more difficult in a chart, but all at once it's very logical if you're looking at your work on your needles.

REPEATS AND SLEEVES

On the traveling stitch and star charts shown here, the repeats are, as usual, framed in red, divided with a vertical dotted line to illustrate how the stitches should be divided over the knitting needles if the pattern is to be used for the sleeves. For a sleeve, when working in the round, place one half of the repeat on Needle 1 (that is, from the red vertical line on the right side of the chart to the dotted line). Place the rest of the repeat on Needle 2. Divide the remaining stitches the same way over Needles 3 and 4.

M-1
Place: Idestrup, Falster.
Repeat: 6 sts x 12 rows/rnds.

M-2
Place: Unknown.
Repeat: 8 sts x 16 rows/rnds.

M-3
Place: North Ørslev, Falster.
Repeat: 10 sts x 20 rows/rnds.

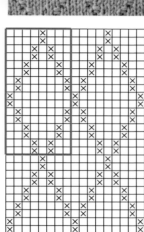

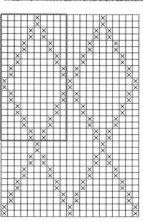

M-4
Place: Kraghave, Falster.
Repeat: 16 sts x 40 rows/rnds.

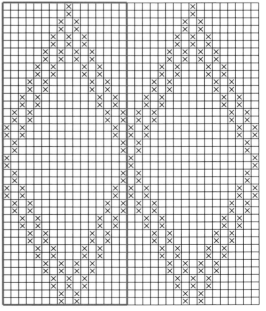

M-5

Place: Brarup, Falster.

Repeat: 14 sts x 24 rows/rnds.

M-6

Place: Brarup, Falster.

Repeat: 20 sts x 36 rows/rnds.

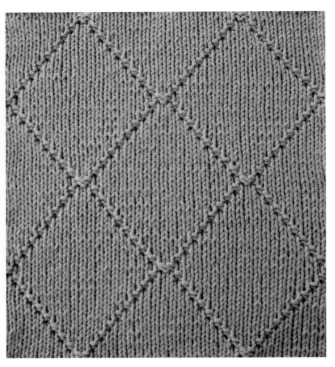

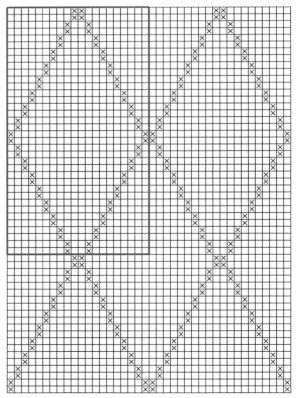

M-7

Place: Toreby, Lolland.

Repeat: 72 sts x 72 rows/rnds.

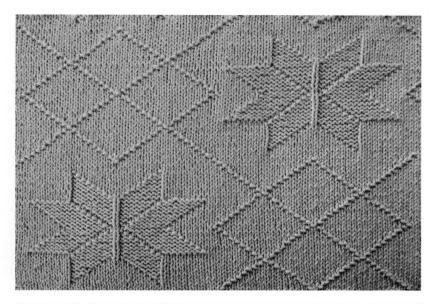

M-8

Place: Unknown.

Repeat: 14 sts x 18 rows/rnds.

M-9

Place: North Ørslev, Falster.

Repeat: 42 sts x 42 rows/rnds.

NOTE: *This pattern should be worked in the round so the rows/rounds with the horizontal stitches can always be worked on the right side.*

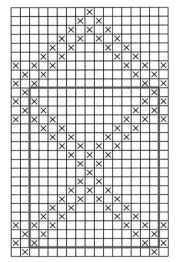

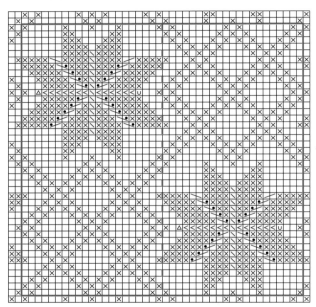

M-10

Place: Hillerød, Zealand.

Repeat: 14 sts x 14 rows/rnds.

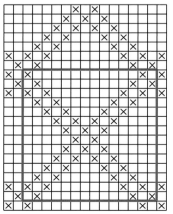

M-11

Place: Bruserup, South Falster.
Repeat: 66 sts x 66 rows/rnds.

M-12

Place: Probably Falster.
Repeat: 72 sts x 72 rows/rnds.

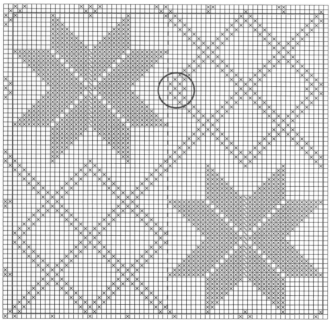

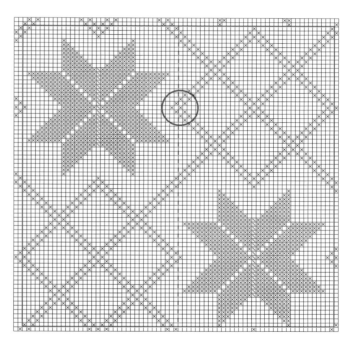

These two designs are almost exactly alike. The one difference is encircled.

M-13

Place: Unknown.

Repeat: 54 sts x 52 rows/rnds.

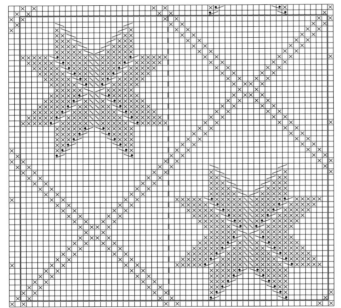

M-14

Place: Rodeminde, Falster.

Repeat: 54 sts x 56 rows/rnds.

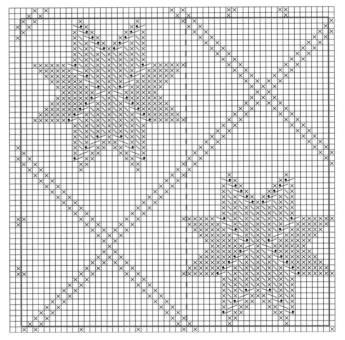

M-15

Place: Unknown.

Repeat: 58 sts x 56 rows/rnds.

M-16

Place: Hillerød, Zealand.

Repeat: 14 sts x 26 rows/rnds.

M-17

Place: Vejringe, Falster.
Repeat: 46 sts x 58 rows/rnds.

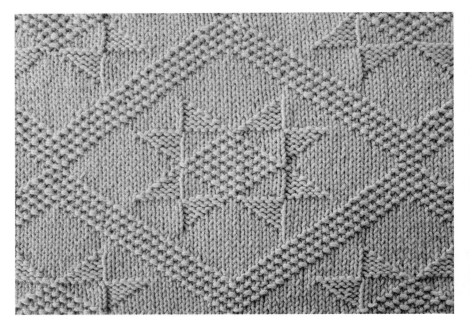

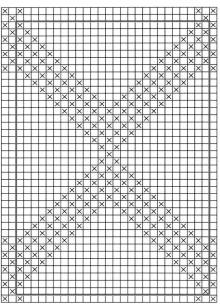

M-18

Place: Vejringe, Falster.
Repeat: 26 sts x 38 rows/rnds.

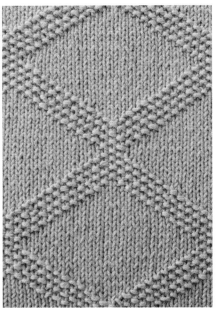

M-19

Place: Stokkemarke, Lolland.
Repeat: 4 sts x 4 rows/rnds (top of chart).
Repeat: 16 sts x 14 rows/rnds (bottom of chart).

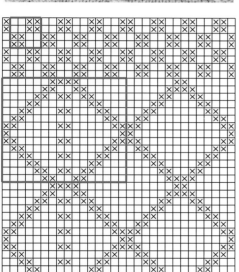

M-20

Place: Nakskov, Lolland.
Repeat: 64 sts x 62 rows/rnds.

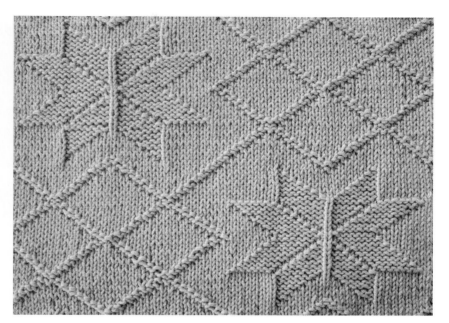

M-21

Place: Sakskøbing, Lolland.

Repeat: 58 sts x 66 rows/rnds.

M-22

Place: Nysted, Lolland.

Repeat: 50 sts x 56 rows/rnds.

M-23

Place: Toreby, Lolland.

Repeat: 48 sts x 46 rows/rnds.

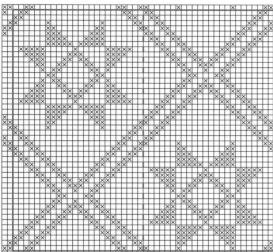

M-24

Place: Moseby, Falster.

Repeat: 50 sts x 60 rows/rnds.

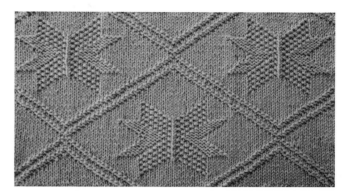

M-25

Place: North Vedby, Falster.

Repeat: 29 sts x 38 rows/rnds.

M-26

Place: Unknown.

Repeat: 16 sts x 24 rows/rnds.

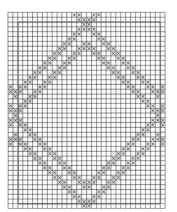

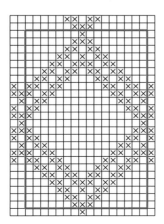

M-27

Place: Unknown.

Repeat: 46 sts x 56 rows/rnds.

Only the stars are different on M-27 and M-28.

M-28

Place: Unknown.

Repeat: 46 sts x 56 rows/rnds.

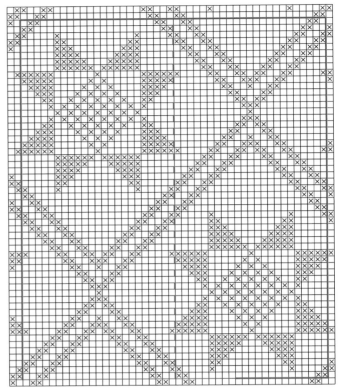

M-29

Place: Undoubtedly Falster. Conserved in Seattle, USA.
Repeat: 60 sts x 68 rows/rnds.

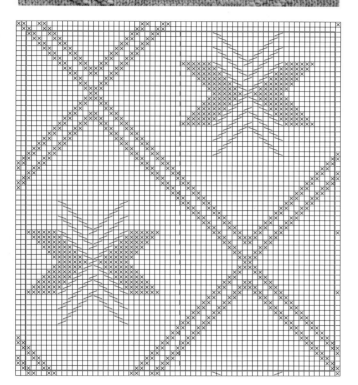

M-30

Place: South Falster.
Repeat: 38 sts x 38 rows/rnds + 11 rows/rnds (at bottom).

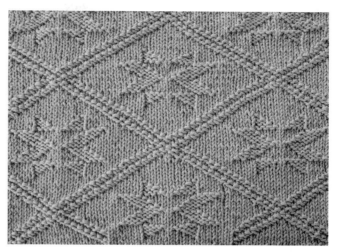

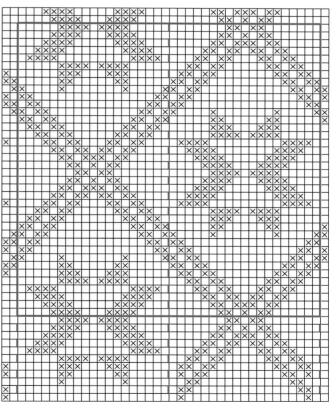

NOTE: *The sleeves, from which this pattern came, began as for 1st row of chart.*

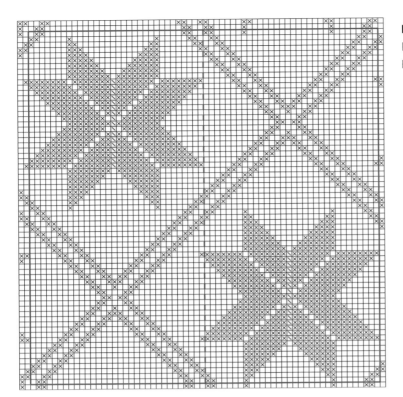

M-31

Place: Nykøbing, Falster.

Repeat: 64 sts x 67 rows/rnds.

M-32

Place: Unknown but undoubtedly Lolland.

Repeat: 52 sts x 62 rows/rnds.

M-33

Place: North Alslev Falster.

Repeat: 52 sts x 62 rows/rnds.

M-34

Place: Karleby, Falster.

Repeat: 58 sts x 76 rows/rnds.

M-35

Place: Aastrup, Falster.

Repeat: 58 sts x 62 rows/rnds.

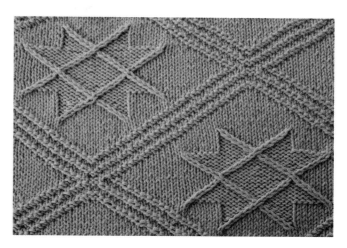

M-36

Place: Sakskøbing, Lolland.

Repeat: 58 sts x 76 rows/rnds.

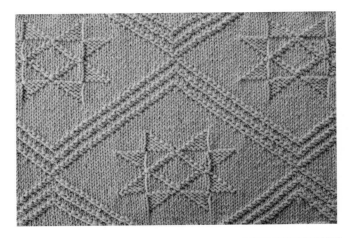

M-37

Place: Toreby, Lolland.

Repeat: 50 sts x 62 rows/rnds.

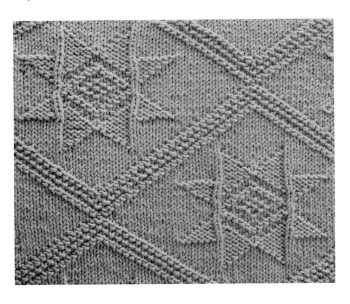

MAIN PATTERNS

M-38

Place: Stubbekøbing, Lolland.
Repeat: 27 sts x 50 rows/rnds.

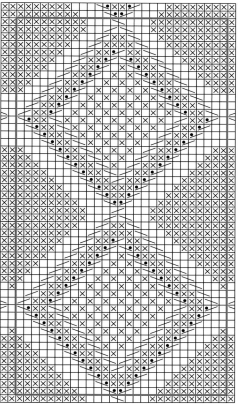

M-39

Place: Nykøbing, Falster.
Repeat: 26 sts x 32 rows/rnds.

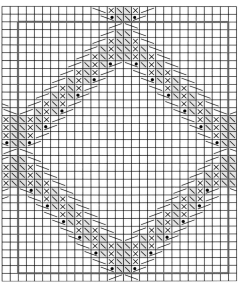

EDGE PATTERNS

Night sweaters have special edge patterns at the lower parts of the sleeves and body. They differ from the main patterns—preferably with two different patterns on, respectively, the body and sleeves. The bottom edges can be combined with a braid, which reinforces the cast-on. The sleeve cuffs are typically knitted in the round, while the edges on the back and front can be knitted back and forth separately and then joined so the night sweater has a split at each side. Depending on whether the edges are narrow or wide, the slit may be long or short.

Many of the edge patterns can be found in several variations but I have chosen the ones used most. One pattern, such as the block (E-7, E-8 and E-9), can be found in many variations with differing stitch counts and rows per block.

Some of the patterns are pretty on both the right and wrong sides. So, they usually can be seen on both sides (see, for example, E-10 and E-11). Other patterns, namely the diagonal ones, can be mirror-imaged, as for E-35, E-36, and E-37.

The sweater to the right is probably from Kærum on West Fyn (KMO/20/1991). The block pattern borders the lower edge of the body, while the sleeve cuffs and neck are edged with ribbing (E-10).

SLEEVE LOWER EDGES
Sleeves are most often edged with k2, p2 ribbing (E-1) or k1tbl, p1 (E-4). You'll find twisted rib on several other edges, including on E-12 and E-18, on sweaters with biased ribbing. See E-33, E-35, and E-36 for biased ribbed edgings.

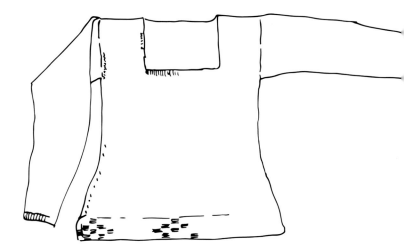

EDGES ON THE BODY
Falster sweaters are most often edged with k2, p2 ribbing (E-1). Curiously enough, there are no k1, p1 ribbed edges, although it's a popular edging nowadays. None of the sweaters have twisted stitches in the lower edge of the body. Several sweaters simply have all garter stitch bottom bands.

In patterns where there are vertical stockinette stitches (E-14, for example), twisted knit is often used. In some instances, I chose to work regular knit but used twisted knit in other places.

REPEATS
Stitch Count: The repeat, framed in red, is repeated across the width. If you want the panels to be symmetrical on each side, in many cases, you'll need to add some stitches. These are indicated by + (for example, +2 sts).
Row Count: The repeat framed in red is to be repeated in height.

E-1
Multiple of 4 sts + 2.
Repeat: 4 sts x 1 row/rnd.

E-2
Multiple of 6 sts + 3.
Repeat: 6 sts x 1 row/rnd.

E-3
Multiple of 8 sts + 4.
Repeat: 8 sts x 1 row/rnd.

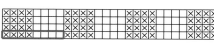

E-4
Multiple of 2 sts + 1.
Repeat: 2 sts x 1 row/rnd.

E-5
Multiple of 4 sts + 2.
Repeat: 4 sts x 1 row/rnd.

E-6
Multiple of 2 sts + 1.
Repeat: 2 sts x 2 rows/rnds.

E-7
Multiple of 4 sts + 2.
Repeat: 4 sts x 1 rows/rnds.

E-8
Multiple of 6 sts + 3.
Repeat: 6 sts x 6 rows/rnds.

E-9
Multiple of 8 sts + 4.
Repeat: 8 sts x 8 rows/rnds.

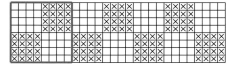

E-10 and E-11

Multiple of 2 sts + 1.

Repeat: 2 sts x 2 rows/rnds.

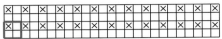

E-12 and E-13

Multiple of 3 sts + 2.

Repeat: 3 sts x 2 rows/rnds.

E-14 and E-15

Multiple of 4 sts + 2.

Repeat: 4 sts x 2 rows/rnds.

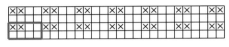

E-16 and E-17

Multiple of 4 sts + 2.

Repeat: 4 sts x 4 rows/rnds.

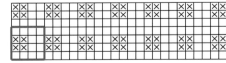

E-18 and E-19

Multiple of 3 sts + 2.
Repeat: 3 sts x 4 rows/rnds.

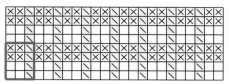

E-20 and E-21

Multiple of 6 sts + 2.
Repeat: 6 sts x 4 rows/rnds.

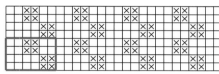

E-22 and E-23

Multiple of 6 sts + 4.
Repeat: 6 sts x 4 rows/rnds.

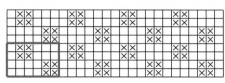

E-24 and E-25

Multiple of 8 sts.
Repeat: 8 sts x 8 rows/rnds.

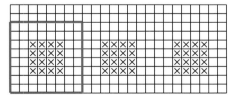

E-26

Multiple of 3 sts.
Repeat: 3 sts x 2 rows/rnds.

E-27

Multiple of 4 sts + 1.
Repeat: 4 sts x 2 rows/rnds.

E-28

Multiple of 6 sts + 1.
Repeat: 6 sts x 4 rows/rnds.

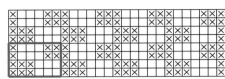

The pattern looks the same on both sides.

E-29

Repeat: 5 sts x 3 rows/rnds.
Repeat: 5 sts x 4 rows/rnds.

A   B

*This motif is a group of 2 patterns.
Worked together, the pattern group is a
multiple of 10 sts.*

E-30

Multiple of 10 sts.
Repeat: 10 sts x 6 rows/rnds.

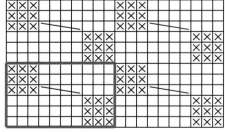

E-31

Multiple of 3 sts + 1.
Repeat: 3 sts x 5 rows/rnds.

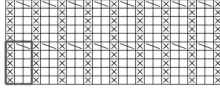

*The pattern above should be worked
in the round. If you work it back and
forth, it's best to space it with either 3
or 5 rows between the cable crossings.*

E-32

Multiple of 6 sts.
Repeat: 6 sts x 4 rows/rnds.

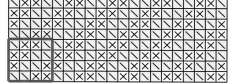

E-33

Multiple of 4 sts.
Repeat: 4 sts x 4 rows/rnds.
This pattern can be mirror-imaged.

E-34

Multiple of 4 sts.
Repeat: 4 sts x 18 rows/rnds.
This pattern can be mirror-imaged.

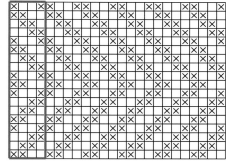

E-35

Multiple of 4 sts + 2.
Repeat: 4 sts x 16 rows/rnds.
This pattern can be mirror-imaged.

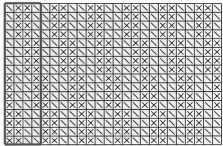

E-36

Multiple of 4 sts + 2.
Repeat: 4 sts x 16 rows/rnds.
This pattern can be mirror-imaged.

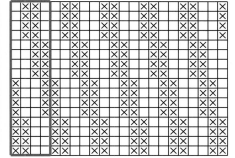

E-37

Multiple of 16 sts.
Repeat: 16 sts x 16 rows/rnds.
This pattern can be mirror-imaged.

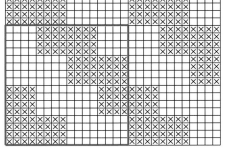

GARMENT INSTRUCTIONS

Hillerød

HILLERØD SWEATER

A number of very exciting traveling stitch and star motif sweaters have been conserved in North Zealand. This is an easy introduction to night sweater knitting because it's so simple and looks so good. Adapted for contemporary styling, the Hillerød sweater features different patterns on the sleeves and body for the horizontal panels and main pattern. The edge patterns on the sleeves are repeated on the shoulders and neck.

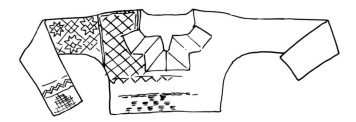

SKILL LEVEL
Beginner

FINISHED MEASUREMENTS
Circumference: 42½ in / 108 cm
Total Length, Back: 19¾ in / 50.5 cm
Total Length, Front: 19 in / 48 cm
Sleeve Length: 17¾ in / 45 cm

MATERIALS
Yarn: CYCA #1 (fingering), Geilsk Cotton and Wool (Bomuld og Uld) (55% wool, 45% cotton, 254 yd/232 m / 50 g; www.nordicyarnimports.com)
Yarn Color and Amount:
Green C3: 7 balls
Needles:
U. S. sizes 0 and 1.5 / 2 mm and 2.5 mm: sets of 5 dpn
U. S. size 0 / 2 mm: straight needles
U. S. size 1.5 / 2.5 mm: 32 in / 80 cm circular
Crochet Hook: U. S. size A / 2.0 mm
Gauge:
28 sts and 44 rnds in main body pattern with U. S. 1.5 / 2.5 mm needles = 4 x 4 in / 10 x 10 cm.
Adjust needle sizes to obtain correct gauge if necessary.

CHARTS AND PATTERNS
Sleeves—horizontal panel and traveling st and star pattern, page 148.
Body—edge pattern, page 149.
Body—horizontal panel and traveling st pattern, page 149
Neck and Shoulders, page 149.

INSTRUCTIONS

Construction: The sleeves and body are worked from the bottom up. The shoulders are joined with 3-needle bind-off and then the sleeves are sewn in. Finally, the neck is edged with a round of crocheted crab stitch.

SLEEVES (MAKE 2 ALIKE)

Lower edge: With U. S. 0 / 2 mm dpn and the **long-tail method**, CO 70 sts. Divide sts as evenly as possible over 4 dpn. Join, being careful not to twist cast-on row; pm for beginning of rnd. Work around in moss st as follows:
Rnd 1: (K1, p1) around.
Rnd 2: Work knit over knit and purl over purl.
Rnd 3: (P1, k1) around.
Rnd 4: Work purl over purl and knit over knit.
Rep these 4 rnds until edging measures 2¾ in / 7 cm.
Knit 1 rnd, increasing 3 sts evenly spaced around = 73 sts.

Horizontal panel: Change to dpn U.S. 1.5 / 2.5 mm and divide the sts over 4 dpn following the chart on page 148.
Needle 1: 14 sts (green section)
Needle 2: 21 sts (yellow section)
Needle 3: 21 sts (pink section)
Needle 4: 17 sts (blue and grey sections)
Knit 12 rnds following the chart for the **horizontal panel**, beginning at the arrow.
Finish with 1 knit rnd.

→

Sleeve, main pattern: Work in traveling st and star pattern from the chart. The 3 gray-shaded sts on the left side of chart continue all the way up the sleeve "seam" as est (see red-framed block for repeat). The large area framed in red on the chart is the main pattern, which is repeated across and up. *At the same time,* increase 1 st before and after the "seam" sts on the 12th rnd, then every 10th rnd 12 times, and finally, every 2nd rnd 13 times. End with 1 knit rnd and then 1 purl rnd = 1 ridge on RS. Loosely BO knitwise.

BODY

Lower edge, front: With straight U. S. 0 / 2 mm needles and the **long-tail method,** CO 152 sts. Work the **lower edge pattern** back and forth, following the chart and text below (**NOTE:** Edge sts are not included on chart).

Row 1 (WS): Knit to last st, p1 (= 1 ridge on RS).

1st Tier of Blocks

Row 2 (RS): Sl 1 knitwise (edge st), begin at A and work to B (= p1, k2), work from B to C (= k8, p8) 9 times, end working C to D (= k2, p1) and end p1 (edge st).
Row 3: Sl 1 knitwise (edge st), Work from D to C (= p1, k1, p1), from C to B (= k8, p8) 9 times, end with B to A (= p1, k1, p1), end end p1 (edge st).
Rep Rows 2-3 through Row 12 of chart. The last row is on RS.

2nd Tier of Blocks

Continue following the chart for 11 more rows. Don't forget to continue the edge sts as est even though they are not on the chart. The last row is on WS.

3rd Tier of Blocks

Rep the 1st tier, with the last row on RS.
End the edge with 1 ridge on RS (= knit on WS except for the 4 outermost sts on each side which continue as est).

Set piece aside.

Lower edge, back: CO and work the first rows as for front.
Block tiers: Begin with the 2nd tier of blocks on the chart (see the top arrow at right side of chart). Work a total of 4 tiers of blocks instead of 3 (= 11 more rows than for front).

Joining without overlapping or twisting (RS): Work the lower edges onto a U.S. 1.5 / 2.5 mm circular as follows, beginning with the front:
Sl 1 knitwise, 2 seed sts (= the 2 outermost sts on each side), knit until 2 seed sts rem on other side, knit last st (edge st) of front edge together with first st (edge st) of back—this stitch will continue in knit/St st all the way up. Now work back sts as for front and end by knitting last st of back together with 1st st of front/edge st—this st also continues all the way in knit/St st (= 2 x 151 sts rem).

Stockinette Rnd 1: Knit the center 146 sts each of front and back, with (2 seed sts, k1, 2 seed sts) over the 5 sts at each side for the seamline.
Rnd 2: Work as for Rnd 1 but decrease 3 sts evenly spaced in each of the stockinette sections (= 2 x 148 sts rem). Work 25 rnds (approx. 2½ in / 6 cm) in stockinette with the 5 side seam sts at each side.

Horizontal panel: Work the bottom 8 rnds of the **horizontal panel** following the chart for the **body** (the side seams are not included on the chart). *K1, 2 seed sts, begin at A and work to B, work from B to C a total of 9 times, from C to D, 2 seed sts*; rep * to * on the back.

Main pattern: Now work the **traveling st pattern** following the chart for the **body** for 51 rnds (3 rep + 9 rnds) = 5¼ in / 13.5 cm. Now divide the piece for back and front at each side. Work each side separately back and forth on the circular.

BACK, CONTINUATION

End the first row (RS) by casting on 1 st (M1-loop) and then continue up as before. The outermost st at each side is an edge st (St st on all rows). Work a total of 140 rows (10 rep) traveling st pattern = 12¾ in / 32 cm. Now work 1 row in traveling st pattern, binding off the center 43 sts. Set piece side.

FRONT, CONTINUATION

Work as for continuation of back until you've worked 106 rows (7 rep + 8 rows) = 9½ in / 24 cm.

Front neck and shoulders: Work the first 10 rows following the chart for the front neck and shoulders. On the next row, BO the center 43 sts and work each side separately until shoulder is complete. Set piece aside.

Work the opposite shoulder to correspond to first.

FINISHING

Join the shoulders with **3-needle BO** (see page 77).

Sew in sleeves.

Work a round of crab st around neck (see page 249).

Split edge and overlap join of edges.

SLEEVES—HORIZONTAL PANEL AND TRAVELING STITCH AND STAR PATTERN

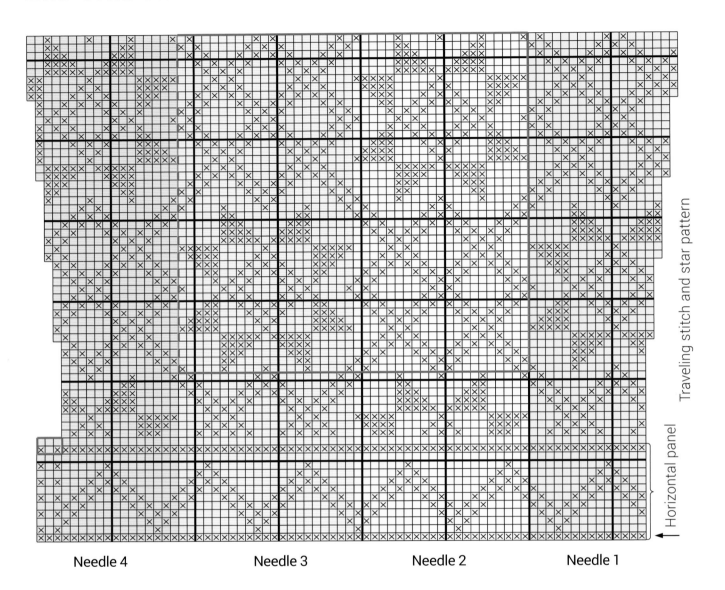

Needle 4   Needle 3   Needle 2   Needle 1

Traveling stitch and star pattern

Horizontal panel

FRONT NECK AND SHOULDERS

Left side/shoulders

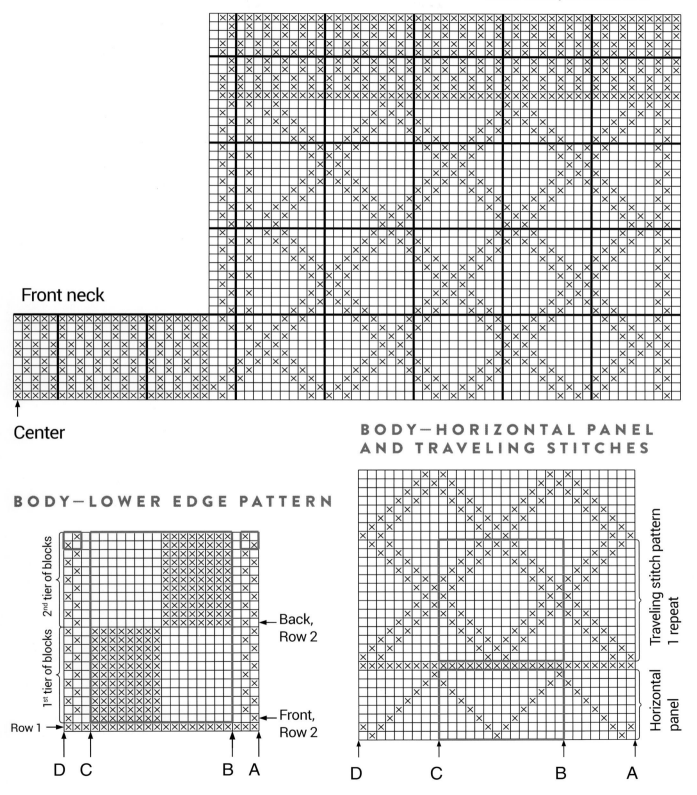

Front neck

Center

BODY—HORIZONTAL PANEL
AND TRAVELING STITCHES

BODY—LOWER EDGE PATTERN

2nd tier of blocks

1st tier of blocks

← Back,
Row 2

Row 1 →

← Front,
Row 2

D   C   B A

Traveling stitch pattern
1 repeat

Horizontal
panel

D   C   B   A

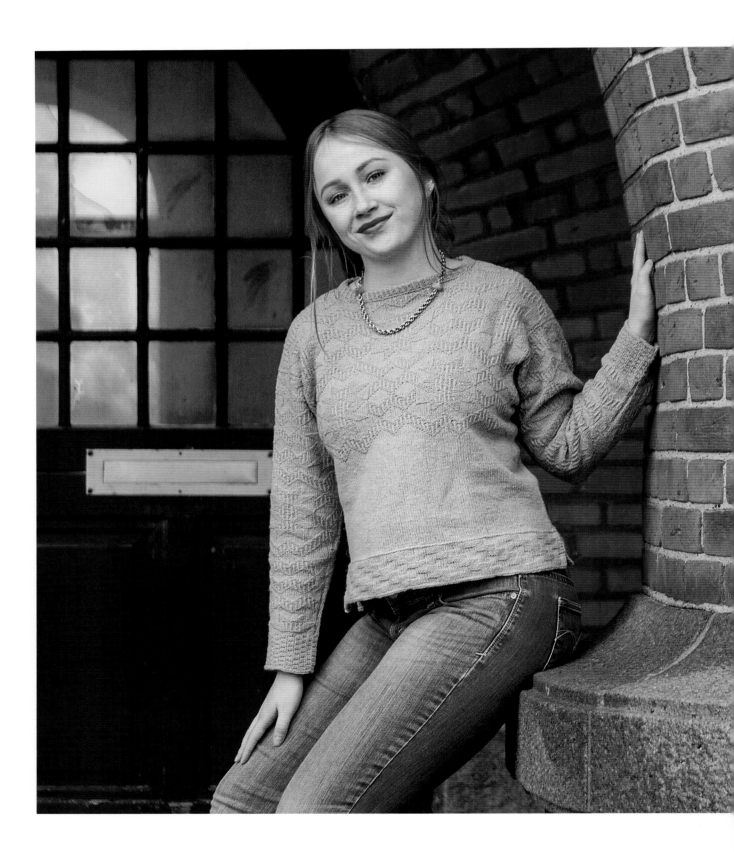

Eskilstrup

ESKILSTRUP SWEATER

A very special sweater had been conserved in the museum storage drawers for some time, one which is not like the other sweaters. It is the Eskilstrup sweater. The main pattern is a complex refinement of the classic traveling stitch and star pattern, which finishes with a distinct pattern section below the arm gussets. Here it is so now you can knit it.

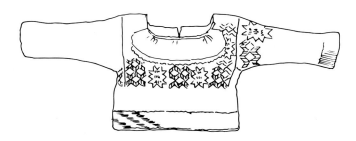

SKILL LEVEL
Intermediate

FINISHED MEASUREMENTS
Circumference: 35½ in / 90 cm straight across below underarm; 37 in / 94 cm in the stockinette section.
Total Length: 21 in / 53 cm
Sleeve Length: 18¼ in / 46 cm

MATERIALS
Yarn:
CYCA #1 (light fingering), Blackhill Linwool (80% wool, 20% linen, 273 yd/250 m / 50 g)
Yarn Color and Amount:
Light Blue (Svinkløv Badehotel) 11: 10 balls
Needles:
U. S. size 1.5 / 2.5 mm: straight needles; 16 or 24 in / 32 in / 40 or 60 cm + 80 cm circulars; set of 5 dpn
Gauge:
30 sts and 40 rnds in St st = 4 x 4 in / 10 x 10 cm.
Adjust needle size to obtain correct gauge if necessary.

CHARTS AND PATTERNS
Edge pattern E-22, page 137
Edge pattern E-37, page 139
Sleeves and Body—traveling st and star pattern, page 156.
Edge pattern E-4, page 135.

INSTRUCTIONS

Construction: The sleeves and body are worked from the bottom up. The shoulders are joined and then the sleeves are sewn in. The neckband is worked last.

TIP: It will be easier to keep track of this somewhat complicated pattern by dividing the sts onto needles in sections. My method is suggested in the pattern.

SLEEVES (MAKE 2 ALIKE)
Lower edge: With dpn, CO 66 sts with German twisted CO method. Divide sts onto 3 dpn: 25 sts on Needle 1, 23 sts on Needle 2, and 25 sts on Needle 3. Use the 4th needle to knit with. Join, being careful not to twist cast-on row; pm for beginning of rnd.
Working in the round, purl 1 rnd, knit 1 rnd and then work **edge pattern E-22** for 2½ in / 6 cm. Knit 1 rnd, increasing to 73 sts as evenly spaced around as possible.

Main pattern: Work traveling st and star pattern (rep framed in green) with 2 purl sts up the sleeve at center of underarm as a sleeve "seam" (not shown on the chart). *At the same time*, increase 1 st before and after the 2 seam sts after 10 rnds and then on every 6th rnd 18 times. When necessary, add another dpn and, at about the 48th rnd, rearrange the st distribution (just move the sts without working them):

Needle 1: 25 sts of star.
Needles 2-3: 23 sts each of zigzag pattern.
Needle 4: first and last 8 sts of chart.
Continue, shifting sts on needles as necessary. Now increase on every 4th rnd 13 times = 137 sts. Work 3 more rnds.

Gusset: Continue in pattern but k2tog with seam sts and work "seam" in stockinette. Increase 1 st on every 2nd rnd before and after the gusset which consists of 3 sts, then 5, then 7, etc. When the gusset has 13 sts, place those sts on a holder. BO rem sleeve sts loosely.

NOTE: If you want the sleeves shorter or longer, work the gusset when you have 13 more rnds (about 1½ in / 4 cm before desired length).

BODY

Lower edge, back: With straight needles, CO 142 sts using long-tail method.
Row 1 (WS): 1 braid knitted under (see page 69).
Row 2 (RS): Knit to last st and end p1.
Row 3 (WS): Work **edge pattern E-37** as follows: Sl 1 knitwise (edge st, not shown on chart), begin at lower left side of chart and work to the right: *K8, p8*; rep * to * and end as shown on chart with k8, p4; end p1 (edge st).
Row 4 (RS): Sl 1 knitwise (edge st), k4, p8, *k8, p8*; rep * to * to last st and end p1 (edge st).

Continue following the chart until you've worked 24 rows. Set piece aside.

Lower edge, front: Work as for back edge.

Overlapping join: Move the sts of each lower edge to a long circular by working on RS as follows: Work the sts of back as est until 5 sts rem, hold these sts behind the first 5 front sts and knit the sets of sts together in pairs (= k2tog with 1st st on each needle). Work across front as est until 5 sts rem; hold these 5 sts in front of 5 first sts of back and join as before (= 274 sts).

Stockinette section: Begin working in the round and purl 1 rnd (= 1 ridge on RS). Continue in stockinette for 5½ in / 14 cm (= knit every rnd). On the last knit rnd, increase 3 sts evenly spaced on each the front and back = 280 sts.

Traveling St and Star Pattern
Rnd 1: Begin at right side of chart with k1 for Side st (right side), k7 and pm (beginning of rnd), k32, p1, k11, p1, k17, k1 (center back), k17, p1, k11, p1, k39, k1 (left side), k39, p1, k11, p1, k17, k1 (center front), k17, p1, k11, p1, k39, p1 (right side) = 280 sts.
Rnds 2-36: Work in pattern following the chart until the side pattern is complete.

Place the 13 sts at each side on a holder for the underarm. Now divide the work for front and back.

BACK, CONTINUATION

Begin at right side of chart, above side pattern (red arrow) and continue the charted pattern, *but* on the first row increase 1 st with M1 (pick up strand between underarm and back st and knit into back loop). End row with M1 increase. These two new sts are edge sts (begin row with sl 1 knitwise) and end with p1); edge sts are not included on chart.
Back neck: Work to back neck on chart; the last row is on WS. Work row and, *at the same time*, place the center 35 sts on a holder.

Left side: Continue following the chart. At back neck (RS), on every other row, BO 4-1-1 sts. Work to end of chart and set piece aside.

Right side: Work as for left side, binding off sts on WS. Set piece aside.

FRONT, CONTINUATION

Work as for back to front neck on chart; the last row is on WS. Work that row and, *at the same time*, place the center 37 sts on a holder.

Right side: Continue following the chart, *but* k2tog tbl inside 1 st on RS rows, at neck edge, a total of 5 times. Work to end of chart and set piece side.

Left side: Work as for right side but end all WS rows (at neck edge) with k2tog, 1 edge st.

FINISHING

Join the shoulders with **3-needle BO** (see page 77). Join gusset sts to underarm using mattress st (or join with 3-needle BO). Sew the rest of each sleeve to armhole.

NECKBAND

Begin by placing the 37 front neck held sts onto short circular and then place the 35 sts of back neck onto circular.

Picking up sts for neck: Beginning at right shoulder, pick up and knit 8 sts in the curve towards back neck, k35 of back neck, pick up and knit 8 sts to left shoulder seam, pick up and knit 14 sts to front neck, k37 (held sts), pick up and knit 14 sts in curve to right shoulder seam = 116 sts total. Purl 1 rnd (= ridge on RS). Knit 1 rnd, decreasing with p2tog at each shoulder seam.
Work 14 rnds in **edge pattern E-4** and then BO loosely in ribbing. Fold the band in half around and sew down on WS.

Slids og samling af kanter med overlap.

SLEEVES AND BODY—TRAVELING
STITCH AND STAR PATTERN

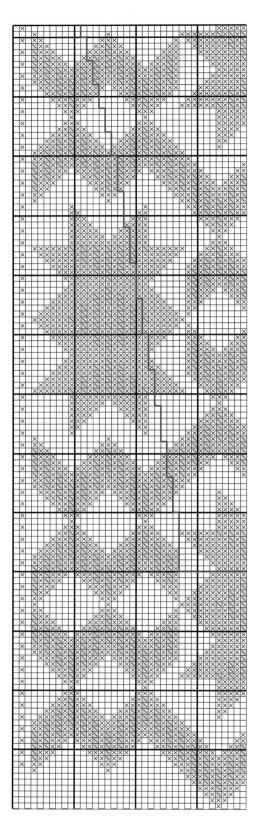

Green frame: Sleeves
Red frame: A complete repeat

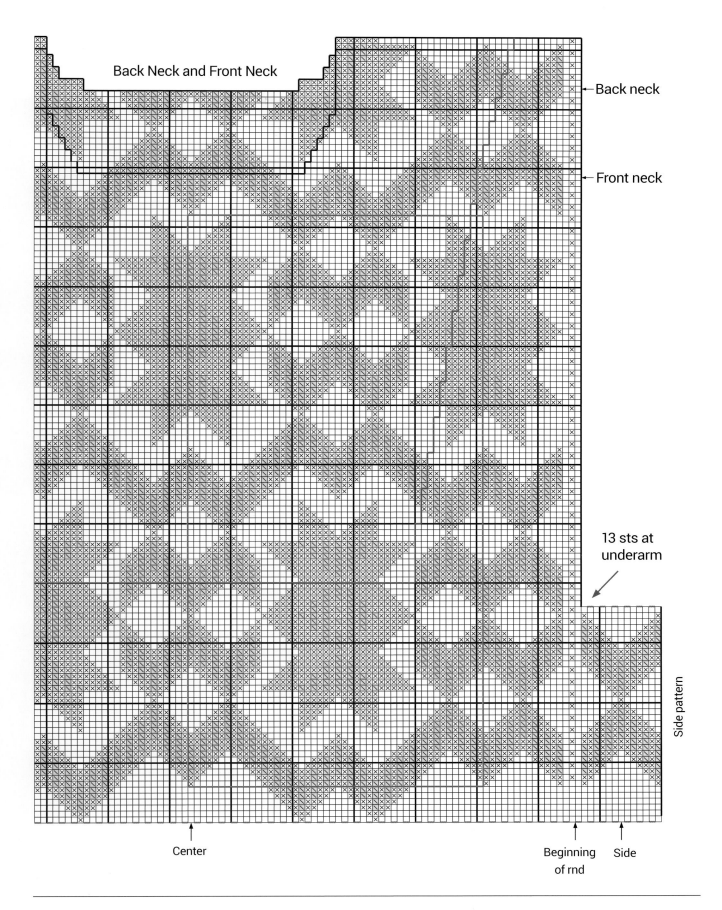

Back Neck and Front Neck

Back neck

Front neck

13 sts at
underarm

Side pattern

Center

Beginning
of rnd

Side

Tunic

TUNIC

You can, of course, adapt the old patterns in ways no would have thought of in the 19th century, as for this Fair Isle-inspired tunic with many colors.

SKILL LEVEL
Experienced

FINISHED MEASUREMENTS
Circumference: 57¼ in / 146 cm
Total Length: 24¾ in / 63 cm

MATERIALS
Yarn:
CYCA #1 (light fingering), Isager Strik Tvinni Tweed (100% pure new wool, 558 yd/510 m / 100 g; www.knitisager.com)
CYCA #1 (light fingering), Isager Strik Tvinni (100% pure new wool, 280 yd/255 m / 50 g; www.knitisager.com)
Yarn Colors and Amounts:
Lavender 25S, Tvinni Tweed: 300 g
Yellow-Green 40, Tvinni: 150 g
Light Yellow 35S, Tvinni Tweed: 100 g
Lime 29S (Tvinni Tweed: 100 g
Small amounts each of:
Olive 15S, Tvinni

Tweed: 50 g
Turquoise 26 Tvinni: 50 g
Tomato 28, Tvinni: 50 g
Red-violet 17, Tvinni: 50 g
NOTE: The yarn amounts will vary depending on your gauge and combination of colors. The tunic photographed here weighs 13.26 ounces / 376 g.
Needles:
U.S. size 1.5 / 2.5 mm: 2 16 in / 40 cm circulars; 2 32 or 40 in / 80 or 100 cm circulars; 3 dpn; cable needle
Gauge:
32 sts and 36 rnds in star pattern = 4 x 4 in / 10 x 10 cm.
Adjust needle size to obtain correct gauge if necessary.

CHARTS AND PATTERNS
Edge pattern E-14, page 136
Traveling st and Star pattern, page 163

INSTRUCTIONS

Construction: The lower edges are worked first and then the piece continues in the round in two-color stranded knitting. The single-color shoulders are last. The openings for the neck and armholes are cut open. The collar and sleeve cuffs are each worked separately and seamed.

BODY

Lower edge, front: With long circular and Lavender, CO 236 sts using long-tail method. Working back and forth, knit to last st and end p1.
Now work **edge pattern E-14** as follows (the edge sts are not included on the chart):
Row 1 (RS): Sl 1 knitwise, knit to last st, end p1.
Row 2 (WS): Sl 1 knitwise, (k2, p2) to last 3 sts, end k2, p1.
Repeat these two rows until edging measures 4 in / 10 cm, ending with a WS row.

Lower edge, back: Work as for front lower edge.

Join with cable twist (RS): Work the two edges onto the long circular as follows: Knit the back until 3 sts rem; place these sts on a cable needle and hold behind work, work the first 3 sts of front as k1, k2tog, pm (left side), work 3 sts from cable needle as k2tog, k1. Knit across front to last 3 sts, place these sts on cable needle and hold in front of work, work first 3 sts of back as k2tog, k1, pm (right side); with sts on cable needle: k2tog, k1 = 468 sts total.
Knit 1 rnd, increasing 36 sts evenly spaced around with about 13 sts between each increase = 504 sts.

→

Side seam stitch: Increase 1 st at right side above marker. This st should always be purled with both colors of the round (it will be almost invisible) and is not worked in pattern.

Main pattern: Work around in **traveling st and star pattern** following the chart. There should be 12 repeats (the entire chart is 42 sts across) on each rnd + the side-seam sts. Begin at the arrow below the chart and work pattern rep 1-7 as shown on chart's right side. Work the first 2 rnds of the 8th pattern rep.

Place the center 63 sts of front on a holder. Continue in the round and, on the first rnd, CO 3 new sts over gap at center neck. Work these 3 "steek" sts in the colors of the rnd, alternating them rnd by rnd. The steek will later be cut open for the neck. End with the top 2 rows of the chart.

Shoulder pattern: Change to Lavender. Begin at the front neck and work 20 rows **edge pattern E-14** back and forth as follows:
Row 1 (RS): Sl 1 knitwise, knit to last st, decreasing 1 st at about center of row; end with p1 = 440 sts.
Row 2 (WS): Sl 1 knitwise, (p2, k2) across, ending with p2, k1.
Row 3 (RS): Sl 1 knitwise, knit to last st, end p1.
Rep Rows 2 -3.

Place all the sts on a holder for later.

Cutting Steeks: Mark the center of the underarm at the center of the 5th pattern rep on each side. Baste down the center of the traveling st and star pattern on the right and left sides to the marker. Place "angel skin" (micro pore tape, which is easy to find) over the basting lines. Machine-stitch a couple of times on each side of the basting lines and in the base, close to the actual pattern. Carefully cut open between the lines. Remove the tape.

Neck steek: Machine-stitch on both sides very close to the steek sts. You don't need the micro pore tape for this steek. Cut the fabric between the machine stitching lines and cut away excess fabric.

Join the shoulders with **3-needle BO** (see page 77).

COLLAR

With Lavender and short circular, CO 168 sts with **long-tail method**. Join, being careful not to twist cast-on row; pm for beginning of rnd. Work **edge pattern E-14** as follows:
Rnd 1 (RS): Knit.
Rnd 2 (WS): (P2, k2) around.
Repeat these 2 rnds until collar measures 6¼ in / 16 cm. Set piece aside.
Place sts of back and front neck onto short circular. K63 of back neck, pick up and knit 21 sts between back and front neck sts, k63 of front neck, and pick up and knit 21 sts to back neck. Purl 1 rnd (= ridge on RS). Now turn work so WS faces out and insert collar into neck opening so the stitches face up, with RS facing RS. Join the sts with **3-needle BO** (page 77).

SLEEVE CUFFS (MAKE 2 ALIKE)

With Lavender and short circular, CO 148 sts with long-tail method. Join and make a 6¼ in / 16 cm long tube in **edge pattern E-14**. Set piece aside.

Place cuff at sleeve edge with RS facing RS and pieces hold with pins or clips. Sew inside the knitting using back stitch, making sure it doesn't draw in. Fold the cuff edge to inside and sew down over seam.

TRAVELING STITCH AND STAR PATTERN

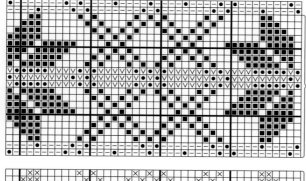

6th pattern repeat

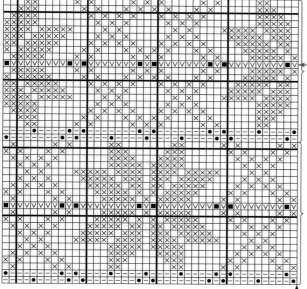

2nd, 4th, and 8th pattern repeats

1st, 3rd, 5th, and 7th pattern repeats

☐ Yellow-Green or desired shading
☒ Lavender
⊙ Red-Violet
■ Tomato
⊟ Olive
▽ Turquoise

The pattern is worked in the round with RS facing in stockinette (knit all rnds).
Each round is worked with two colors.

The background color (blank square) is worked with 3 yellow-green shades sequenced as you like (yellow-green, light green and lime) or with colors you have on hand.

The other colors are worked as shown by the chart symbols.

Frenderup

FRENDERUP SWEATER

In Køge, I found a sweater from Frenderup that reminded me of a contemporary sweater. My version is almost a copy. The points of the stars on the sleeves become one stitch larger for every increase. A simple traveling stitch pattern combines with two edge patterns used on the body and sleeves to embellish the lower edge of the body. The original sweater was cut open for the center front, so I decided to make my sweater with an open front.

SKILL LEVEL
Intermediate

FINISHED MEASUREMENTS
Circumference: 40¼ in / 102 cm
Total Length: 22 in / 56 cm
Sleeve Length: 20½ in / 52 cm

MATERIALS
Yarn:
CYCA #1 (light fingering), Isager Strik Tvinni Tweed (100% pure new wool, 558 yd/510 m / 100 g; www.knitisager.com)
Yarn Color and Amount:
Lime 29S: 300 g
Needles:
U. S. size 1.5 / 2.5 mm: straight needles; set of 5 dpn; 24, 32 or 40 in / 60, 80 or 100 cm circulars
Gauge:
30 sts and 44 rnds in traveling st pattern = 4 x 4 in / 10 x 10 cm.
Adjust needle size to obtain correct gauge if necessary.

CHARTS AND PATTERNS
Edge pattern E-10, page 136
Sleeves—traveling st and star pattern, page 170
Edge pattern E-8, page 135
Body—traveling st pattern, page 172
Edge pattern E-7, page 135

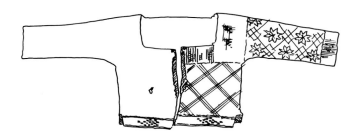

INSTRUCTIONS

Construction: The sleeves and body are worked from the bottom up. The shoulders are joined with **3-needle BO** and then the sleeves are sewn in.

FIRST SLEEVE
Lower edge: With dpn, CO 72 sts with long-tail method. Divide sts evenly onto 4 dpn. Join, being careful not to twist cast-on row; pm for beginning of rnd. Work around in **edge pattern E-10** for 2½ in / 6 cm.
Next, purl 1 rnd (= ridge on RS); knit 1 rnd, increasing evenly spaced around to 84 sts.

Main pattern: Continue with traveling st and star pattern following the chart. For the first tier of the pattern, arrange the sts as follows:
Needle 1: a star;
Needle 2: traveling st pattern;
Needle 3: a star;
Needle 4: traveling st pattern.
On the last rnd of the first tier, increase 1 st (M1-loop = backwards loop, page 67) at each of the short red lines. Continue in charted pattern, increasing on the last rnd of the 2nd, 3rd, and 4th pattern tiers (= 116 sts). Work the 5th and 6th tiers without increasing. →

Gusset: *At the same time* as working 7th tier, make a gusset (not included on chart).
Rnd 1: Work as est to last st, M1-loop increase, k1.
Rnd 2: K1, M1, work rest of rnd. The gusset now has 4 sts.
Rnds 3 and 4: Work to gusset and knit the gusset sts (= gusset is in St st).
Rnd 5: Work to last 2 sts of rnd, M1-loop increase, k2.
Rnd 6: K2, M1, work to end of rnd. The gusset now has 6 sts.
Rnds 7 and 8: Work to gusset and knit the gusset sts.

Continue increasing on each side of the gusset as est; the gusset sts are always knitted. Increase for the gusset throughout tier 7.

BO loosely.

SECOND SLEEVE
Lower edge: Work as for first sleeve.

Main pattern: Now turn the chart a quarter turn so that the patterns will match when the two sleeves are attached. Arrange the sts as follows:
Needle 1: traveling st pattern;
Needle 2: a star;
Needle 3: traveling st pattern;
Needle 4: a star.
Continue as for the first sleeve. As before, inc for the gusset at the end/beginning of respective rnds.

BODY
Lower edge, back: With straight needles, CO 151 sts with long-tail method.
Row 1 (WS): P2 (edge sts at split), knit until 2 sts rem, end p2 (edge sts at split).
Row 2: Knit.
Now begin **edge pattern E-8:**
Row 3 (WS): This is the 1st chart row. Begin at left side of chart and work towards the right: P2 (edge sts at split;

not included on chart), (k3, p3) until 5 sts rem; end k3, p2 (edge sts at split; not included on chart).
Continue in pattern with 2 St sts at each side until you've worked 27 edge patterns (9 rows of blocks). The last row is on WS.
Set piece aside.

Lower edge, left front: With straight needles, CO 80 sts with **long-tail method**. Work Rows 1-2 as for lower edge of back.
Now begin **edge pattern E-8:**
Row 3 (WS): K3 (front edge), (k3, p3) until 5 sts rem; end k3, p2 (edge sts at split; not included on chart).
Row 4 (RS): K2, (p3, k3) to end of row.
Continue in pattern with 2 St sts at split side and k3 at front edge until this piece is same height as for back. Set piece aside.

Lower edge, right front: With straight needles, CO 80 sts with **long-tail method**. Work Rows 1-2 as for lower edge of back.
Now begin **edge pattern E-8:**
Row 3 (WS): P2 (edge sts at split), (k3, p3) until 6 sts rem; end k3, k3 (front edge).
Continue until this piece is same height as for back.

Overlapping join: Work across all 3 edges with long circular (32 or 40 in / 80 or 100 cm) as follows:
(RS): Knit across right front until 2 sts rem. Hold these sts in front of 1st 2 sts of back. Knit the 2 sets of sts together (join first st on each needle with k2tog). Pm (right side) between the two joined sts. Knit across back until 2 sts rem. Hold these sts behind the 1st 2 sts of left front and join the sets of sts as before. Pm (left side) between the 2 joined sts. Knit to end of front = 307 sts.

Ridges: Work back and forth over all the sts:
Row 1 (WS): Knit (= 1 ridge on RS).

Row 2: Knit, decreasing 1 st at the center of each front piece and inc 1 with M1-loop at center of back.
Row 3: Knit (= 1 ridge on RS).

Main pattern: Work in **traveling st pattern** but continue front edges by knitting the first and last 3 sts all the way up.

1st Pattern Row (WS): K3 (front edge), work from B to D (72 sts), from D to E (6 sts, side seam), from B to C (36 sts), from C to D 3 times (108 sts), from D to E (6 sts, side seam), from B to D (72 sts), end with k3 (front edge). This establishes the pattern.
NOTE: The 6 sts at each side are a side pattern running all the way up each side.
Continue up the same way, following chart until you've worked a total of 105 traveling st rows.
End with the last row on chart (WS), but, inc (M1-loop) 1 st before and 1 st after the armhole opening at each side (marked with green lines on the chart).

RIGHT FRONT, CONTINUATION

Place the 152 sts of back and 79 sts of left front on holders. With circular, work right front back and forth, dividing the pattern on a RS row as follows:
K3 (front edge), 25 sts **edge pattern E-10**, 46 sts **edge pattern E-7**, end with 1 st (St st) and 3 sts **side pattern**, 1 edge st (begin all rows at armhole with sl 1 knitwise and end with p1).
Continue as now est for 6¼ in / 16 cm (approx. 68 rows), ending with a WS row.
BO the first 27 sts (above E-10 pattern for front neck). Continue as est over rem sts (the first st at neck now becomes an edge st) until piece measures 3¼ in / 8 cm from neck shaping (approx. 36 rows). Set piece aside.

LEFT FRONT, CONTINUATION

Place sts for left front onto circular and work to correspond to right front. BO for front neck at the beginning of a WS row when at same length as right front.

BACK, CONTINUATION

Place sts for back onto circular and work back and forth. Divide the sts on a RS row as follows:
1 edge st (k1 at beginning of row and p1 at end for all rows), 3 **side pattern** sts as est, 1 St st, 34 sts **edge pattern E-7**, 1 St st, 72 **traveling pattern** sts continue, 1 St st, 34 sts **edge pattern K-7**, 1 St st, 3 **side pattern** sts, 1 edge st.
Continue as est until piece measures 8¾ in / 22 cm (104 rows) after underarm.
BO the center 36 sts and work each side separately.
Left side: Continue in pattern, binding off at beginning of each RS row 4 sts and then 2 sts. Set aside after 2 rows.
Right side: Work to correspond to left side, binding off at neck edge on WS.

FINISHING

Join shoulders with **3-needle BO** (page 77).
Sew in sleeves.

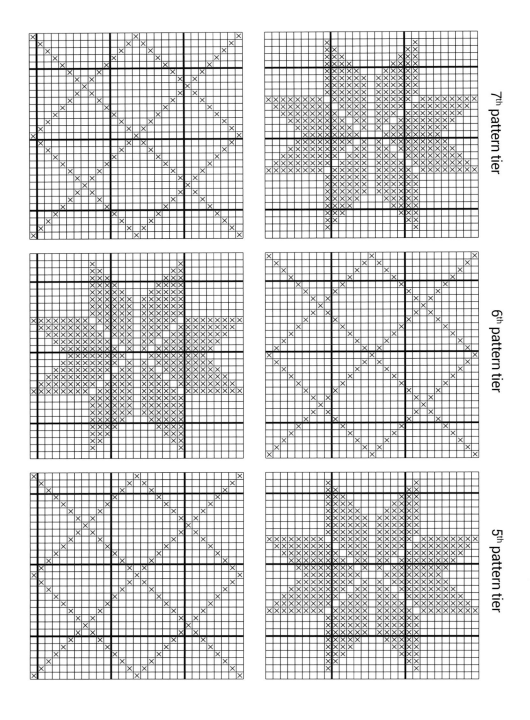

7th pattern tier

6th pattern tier

5th pattern tier

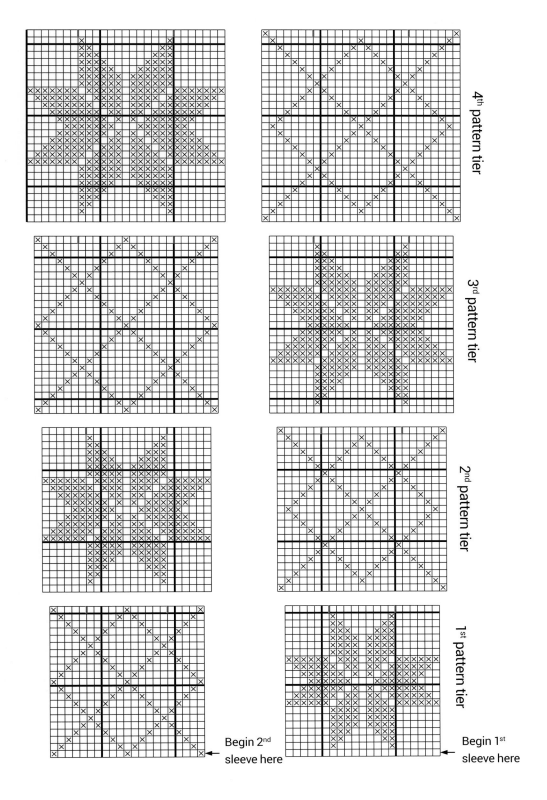

4th pattern tier

3rd pattern tier

2nd pattern tier

1st pattern tier

Begin 2nd
sleeve here

Begin 1st
sleeve here

BODY—TRAVELING STITCH PATTERN

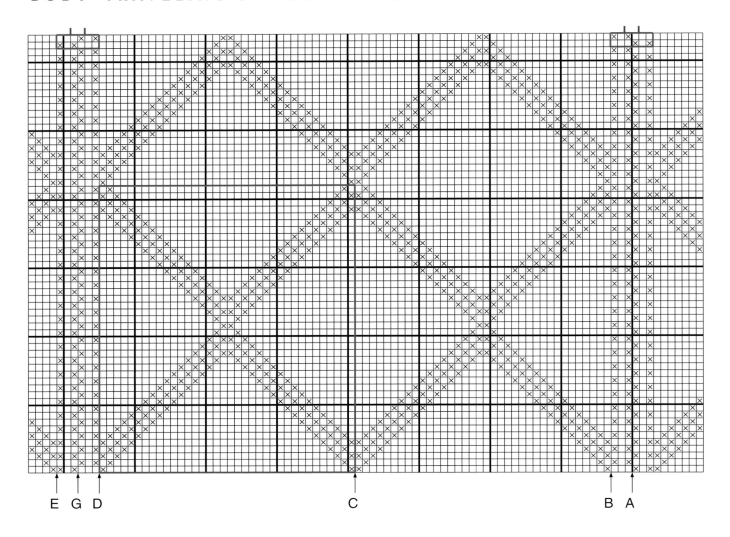

E G D   C   B A

Annie

ANNIE'S SWEATER

Designer: Annie Hansen
Annie began her sweater design with the advice on page 234: She first found a sweater that fitted, measured it, chose the yarn and pattern, knitted swatches and measured the gauge. After that, she calculated the number of stitches and rows, sketched a design and decided how to arrange the patterns. Annie chose to knit her own night sweater and here's her design.

SKILL LEVEL
Intermediate

FINISHED MEASUREMENTS
Circumference: 37¾ in / 96 cm
Total Length: 19 in / 48 cm
Sleeve Length (3/4 length sleeves):
15½ in / 39 cm

MATERIALS
Yarn:
CYCA #1 (light fingering), Blackhill Cotton-Wool (50% cotton, 50% Merino wool, 252 yd/230 m / 50 g)
Yarn Color and Amount:
Kiwi Green 15: 5 balls
Needles:
U. S. size 1.5 / 2.5 mm: straight needles; set of 5 dpn; 24 in / 60 cm circular
Gauge:
28 sts and 40 rows in St st = 4 x 4 in / 10 x 10 cm
Adjust needle size to obtain correct gauge if necessary.

CHARTS AND PATTERNS
Sleeves—traveling st pattern, page 180
Edge pattern, page 179
Side seam, page 179
Horizontal panel H-5, page 93.
Vertical panel V-26, page 107
Stars S-1, S-9, S-10, and S-12, pages 83-84

INSTRUCTIONS

Construction: The sleeves and body are worked from the bottom up. The shoulders are joined with **3-needle BO** and then the sleeves are sewn in.

SLEEVES (MAKE 2 ALIKE)
Lower edge: With dpn, CO 60 sts with **German twisted cast-on** (page 65). Divide sts evenly onto 4 dpn. Join, being careful not to twist cast-on row; pm for beginning of rnd. Purl 1 rnd (= ridge on RS).
Work **edge pattern** (see chart on page 179) for 1½ in / 4 cm. End on either Row 4 or Row 8 of pattern.
Purl 1 rnd (= ridge on RS), increasing 1 st at beginning of rnd. This st will be the sleeve "seam" and is worked in St st all the way up.

Main pattern: Work in **traveling st pattern** following the chart for the rest of the sleeve (the chart shows only a half sleeve). *At the same time*, inc 1 st (with M1-loop) before and after the sleeve "seam" on every 8th rnd.

When sleeve is 15½ in / 39 cm long (or desired length), BO.

→

BODY

Lower edge, back: With straight needles, CO 130 sts with **German twisted CO**. Work in **edge pattern** for 2½ in / 6 cm as follows:

Row 1 (RS): (P1, k2) to last st, end p1.

Continue following the chart. There are no edge sts—the pattern is continuous across. End with either Row 4 or 8 of chart.

Set piece aside.

Lower edge, front: Work as for back lower edge.

Overlapping join: Now join the two lower edge pieces on a circular. With RS facing: Knit across front sts until 4 sts rem. Hold the 1st 4 sts of back behind the last 4 sts of front. *P2tog with the 1st st of each needle, sl next st of front, knit next st of front together with 2 first sts of back and pass slipped st over. End by purling the 1st st of each needle together (8 sts are now reduced to 3 sts)*. Knit sts of back until 4 sts rem, place the last 4 sts on back behind 1st 4 sts of front (the first ones knitted); rep * to * = 250 sts.

Now work in the round. Work the side seam sts following the chart all the way up. The main pattern is worked between the side panels.

Purl 1 rnd and then knit 1 rnd, increasing 5 sts on front and 5 sts on back evenly spaced around.

Horizontal panel: Work **horizontal panel H-5**, beginning 6 sts in on the chart.

Knit 1 rnd, purl 1 rnd above the panel.

Main pattern: Begin after a side seam with the following arrangement of patterns (both front and back):
*K5 (St st), 3 seed sts, 4 St sts, 13 sts **vertical panel V-26**, 4 St sts, 3 seed sts, 12 St sts, 33 St sts (up to first star, see below), 12 St sts, 3 seed sts, 4 St sts, 13 sts **vertical panel V-26**, 4 St sts, 3 seed sts, 5 St sts, 9 sts side seam*; rep * to *.

Work 8 rnds straight up in pattern as est. Now also work stars at **center front** and **center back** (see photo on page 174):

First star: S-10 (33 sts/33 rnds), 10 rnds St st with main pattern as before.

Second star: S-1 (33 sts/33 rnds), 10 rnds St st.

Third star: S-9 (33 sts/33 rnds), 10 rnds St st.

Fourth star: S-12 (17 sts/17 rnds), 7 rnds St st.

At the same time, when beginning the 3rd star and with piece measuring 11¾ in / 30 cm, work 1 rnd, binding off the center st of each side seam. Now divide piece and work front and back separately.

BACK, CONTINUATION

Work back and forth on circular in the same patterns as before, but change the outermost st at each side to an **edge st** (begin row with sl 1 knitwise, end with p1).

After completing the 4th star + 7 rows St st, continue side patterns as est but work the **edge pattern** over the center 49 sts for neck:

Begin on RS with Row 4 of chart: P1, *2 traveling sts, p1*; rep * to * a total of 16 times.

After 8 rows, BO the center 37 sts and work each side separately.

Right side: K2tog inside edge st after 1 row, work 1 more row and set piece aside.

Left side: Work to correspond to right side but decrease when 3 sts rem at neck edge on RS: sl 1 purlwise, k1, psso.

FRONT, CONTINUATION

Work as for back until the 3rd star + 10 rows St st are complete. Work 10 rows in **edge pattern** over the center 49 sts as for back. Next, on RS, BO the center 35 sts and work each side separately.

Right side: After 3 rows, k2tog inside the edge st, and then rep once more. Work straight up until piece measures 19 in / 48 cm and neck depth is 2½ in / 6 cm. Place pieces on holder.

Left side: Work to correspond to right side but decrease when 3 sts rem at neck edge on RS: sl 1 knitwise, k1, psso.

FINISHING

Join shoulders with **3-needle BO** (page 77) but work with RS facing out (WS of back and front facing each other). This makes a decorative line along the shoulder.

Sew in sleeves.

Split edge and overlapped edges at join.
A side seam is worked above the join.

EDGE PATTERN

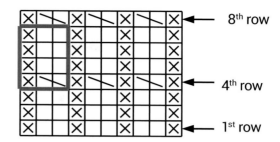

← 8ᵗʰ row

← 4ᵗʰ row

← 1ˢᵗ row

SIDE SEAM

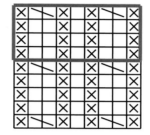

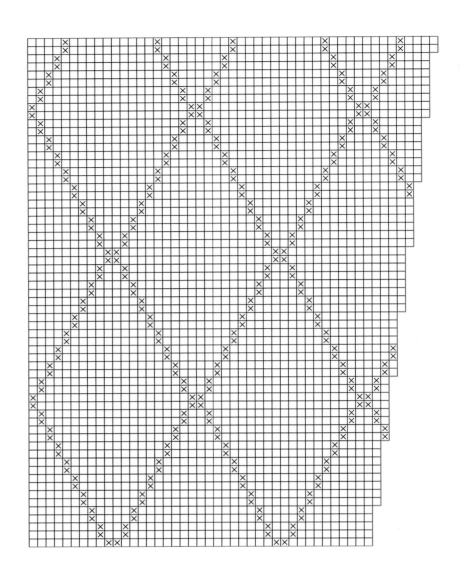

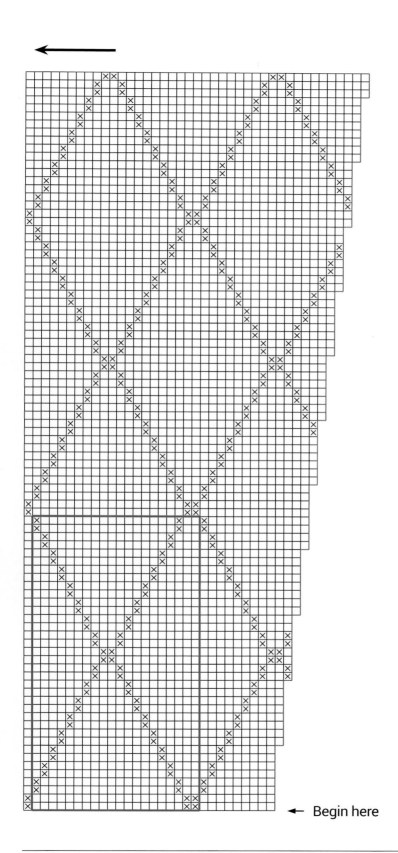

← Begin here

Fantasy

FANTASY SWEATER

I used a few special patterns for this sweater. A side panel goes all the way up the body and out under the sleeves. Finally, chain stitch embroidery with colorful leftover yarns enhances the stars.

SKILL LEVEL
Intermediate

FINISHED MEASUREMENTS
Circumference: 41 in / 104 cm
Total Length: 21¼ in / 54 cm

MATERIALS
Yarn:
CYCA #1 (fingering), Harrisville Shetland (100% virgin wool, 217 yd/210 m / 50 g; www.harrisville.com)

Yarn Color and Amount:
Goldenrod Yellow 61: 400 g

Needles:
U. S. size 2.5 / 3 mm: straight needles; 24 and 32 in / 60 and 80 cm circulars; set of 5 dpn; cable needle

Gauge:
23½ sts and 42½ rnds in traveling st pattern on back/front = 4 x 4 in / 10 x 10 cm.
Adjust needle size to obtain correct gauge if necessary.

CHARTS AND PATTERNS
Edge pattern, page 187
Body, page 188
Sleeves—traveling st and star pattern, page 190

INSTRUCTIONS

Construction:
The body is worked from the bottom up. The shoulders are joined with **3-needle BO**. The sleeves are worked from the top down. Finally, the neckband is knitted on.

BODY
Lower edge, front: With straight needles, CO 122 sts with **long-tail method**.
Work back and forth in **edge pattern** as follows:
Row 1 (WS): K1 (edge st), p2 (not included on chart). Begin at arrow at left side and work following chart: K3, p2, (k4, p2) until 6 sts rem, k3, end with p2, p1 (edge st, not on chart).
Row 2 (RS): Sl 1 knitwise (edge st), k2, p3, k2, (p4, k2) until 6 sts rem, p3, end with k2 and p1 (edge st).
Continue with 1 edge st and 2 St sts at each side and the edge pattern following the chart in between until piece measures 2¾ in / 7 cm. Set piece aside.

Lower edge, back: Work as for front. Do not cut yarn but continue with join.

Join with cable twist: With RS facing, knit the 2 edge bands onto circular as follows: Knit across back until 3 sts rem, *at the same time* increasing 14 sts evenly spaced across. Place the last 3 sts of back on cable needle and hold behind work; knit 1st 3 sts of front and then k3 from cable needle. Knit across front until 3 sts rem, *at the same time* increasing 14 sts evenly spaced across. Hold last 3 sts of front in front of work, knit first 3 sts of back and then k3 from front. K8 and pm for beginning of rnd.

→

Main pattern: Now work in the round following the chart for the **body**. Begin at lower right of chart and work towards left. Work chart once for the back and once for the front. Continue as est to underarm and piece measures 11¾ in / 30 cm. Place the side panel's 16 sts on a holder at each side.

BACK, CONTINUATION

Work back and forth, continuing as est straight up, but, on the 1st row, increase 1 st at each side. The new sts are edge sts (begin row with sl 1 knitwise and end with p1). When piece measures 21¾ in / 55 cm, begin neck.

Neck: BO the center 36 sts loosely. The sts rem on each side of the bind-off are the shoulders. Place these sts on a holder.

FRONT, CONTINUATION

Work as for back, but, when piece measures 18¼ in / 46 cm, BO the center 14 sts for neck. Now work each side separately.

Right side: At beginning of all RS rows, at neck edge, BO 3-3-4-1-1-1 sts and then continue without shaping until piece is same length as back. End with a WS row.

Shape shoulder with short rows: Continue following the chart to the last 10 sts, turn, yo, and complete row. On RS, work until 11 sts rem before previous turn; turn, yo and complete row. On RS, work until 11 sts rem before previous turn; turn, yo and complete row, ending at neck edge. Cut yarn.

Finish shoulder shaping on RS: Knit and, *at the same time*, join each yo with the following st (k2tog).

Shoulder pattern:
Shoulder Row 1 (WS): Sl 1 knitwise, knit to last st, end p1.
Shoulder Row 2 (RS): Sl 1 knitwise, purl to last st, end p1.
Shoulder Row 3 (WS): Sl 1 knitwise, purl to last st, end p1.
Shoulder Row 4 (RS): Sl 1 knitwise, knit to last st, end p1.

Shoulder Row 5 (WS): Sl 1 knitwise, knit to last st, end p1.
Shoulder Row 6 (RS): Sl 1 knitwise, purl to last st, end p1.
Set piece aside.

Left side: Work as for right side but BO on WS (at neck edge). End with a RS row.
Shape shoulder: Continue following the chart to the last 10 sts, turn, yo, and complete row. On WS, work until 11 sts rem before previous turn; turn, yo and complete row. On WS, work until 11 sts rem before previous turn; turn, yo and complete row, ending at neck edge. Cut yarn.

Finish shoulder shaping on WS: Purl and, *at the same time*, join each yo with the following st (p2tog).
Join shoulders with **3-needle BO** (page 77).

NECKBAND

Place the 36 back neck sts on a circular. Pick up and knit sts around neck: 3 sts at left shoulder, 3 sts along shoulder pattern, 25 sts at rounding of front neck, 14 sts at front neck, 25 sts along front neck rounding, 3 sts along shoulder pattern, and 3 sts to back neck = 112 sts total.
Purl 1 rnd.
K-CO 18 sts as an extension of the 112 sts on left needle.
Row 1 (RS): Work the 18 new sts and the first of the 112 sts: k15, p2, p2tog; turn.
By working p2tog at the end of every RS row, the 112 sts will become fewer and fewer until, finally, they disappear—then the neckband is finished!
Row 2 (WS): Sl 1 knitwise, p1, k1, purl to end of row.
Row 3 (RS): Sl 1 knitwise, p15, p2tog; turn.
Row 4 (WS): Sl 1 knitwise, p1, knit to last st, end p1.
Row 5 (RS): Sl 1 knitwise, k14, p2, p2tog; turn.
Rep Rows 2-5 until only 18 rem (the neckband sts).

Sew the cast-on edge and the last 18 sts (BO the 18 sts first) together. Fold the band doubled to WS and sew down.

RIGHT SLEEVE

Main pattern: Place the 16 sts of side pattern on 24 in / 60 cm circular and pick up and knit sts around armhole: 58 sts along back of armhole to shoulder (pick up and knit 2 sts in every 3rd edge st = 1 st under the top loop and 1 st under both loops), 4 sts along shoulder pattern, and 58 sts on front of armhole = 136 sts total.

Rnd 1: Continue around with the 16 sts of **side panel** as est and purl the rem 120 sts.
Rnd 2: Work **side panel** (not on chart), and then work 120 sts following chart, beginning at A and ending at B.
Rnd 3 (decrease rnd): Work 15 **side panel** sts, p2tog (last st of side panel and 1st st of charted sts); work **traveling st and star pattern** for sleeve (begin from chart 1 st in) to last chart st, p2tog (last chart st with 1st st of side panel).

Continue **side pattern** all the way to the edge and work in **traveling st and star pattern** over rem sts. *At the same time,* decrease as before (as for Rnd 3) on every other rnd a total of 18 times and then on every 6th rnd to desired length— or until 3 in / 7.5 cm before edge. Change to dpn when necessary.

Lower sleeve edge: Knit 1 rnd, decreasing to 54 sts evenly spaced around.
Purl 3 rnds and then knit 1 rnd.
Now work 24 rnds in charted **edge pattern**, working the repeat framed in red.
BO.

LEFT SLEEVE

Work as for right sleeve, but, after the 16 sts of side pattern, pick up and knit sts along front and then along back of armhole.

EMBROIDERY

If desired, embroider with a variety of colors. Work chain st in the traveling st diamonds in the middle of some of the stars.

EDGE PATTERN

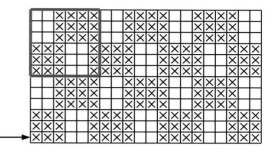

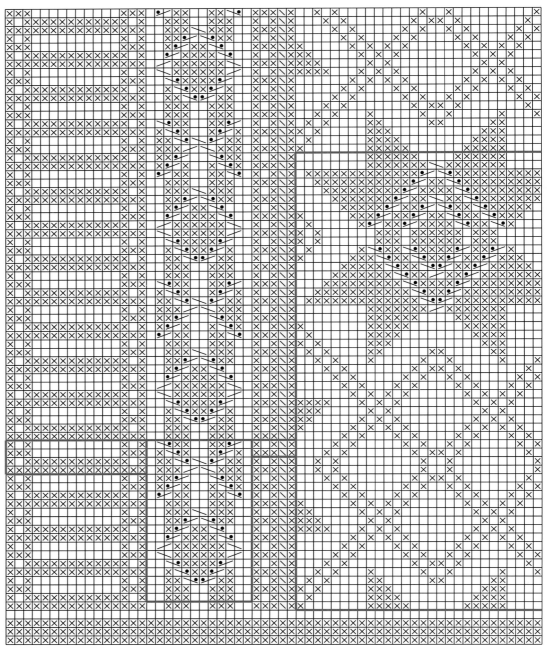

Side pattern   Vertical   Vertical
                      panel   panel
                      12 sts   5 sts

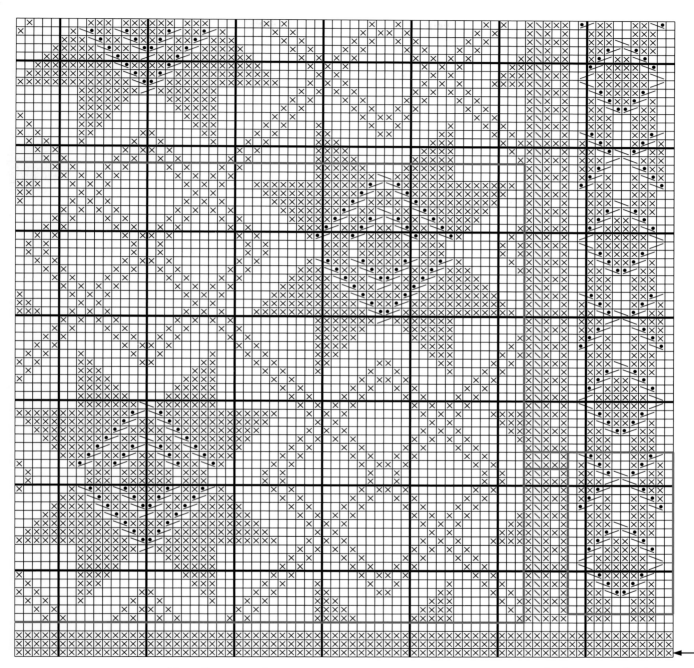

Traveling st and star pattern

Vertical
panel
5 sts

Vertical
panel
12 sts

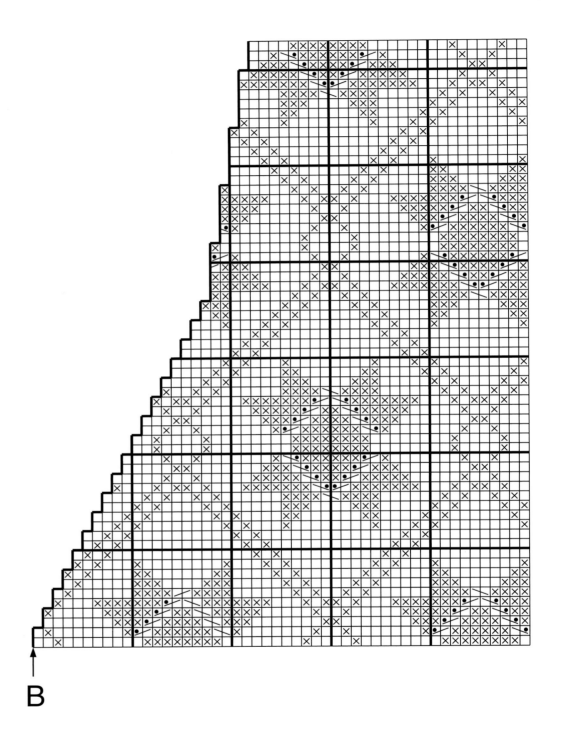

B

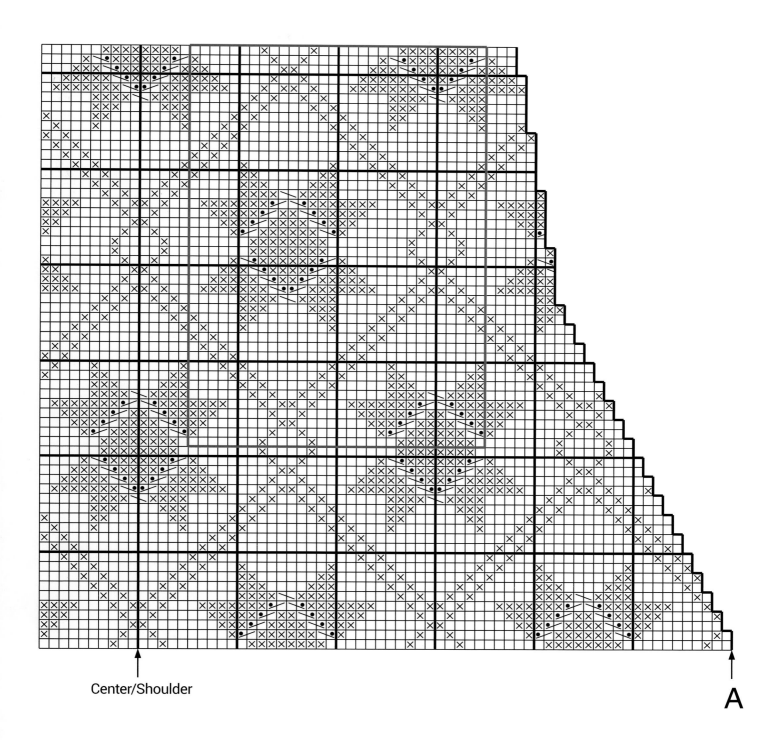

Center/Shoulder

A

aastrup

AASTRUP SWEATER

Maren Smed from Aastrup on northeast Falster knitted and wore the sweater which was the inspiration for this contemporary version. It is a typical North Falster design with vertical traveling stitch and star patterns flanked by vertical panels on each side and a stockinette section in the middle. It is also distinct to North Falster in that the shoulder seams are at the front and not on the shoulder lines.

SKILL LEVEL
Intermediate

FINISHED MEASUREMENTS
Circumference: 41¾ in / 106 cm
Total Length: 17 in / 43 cm
Sleeve Length: 10¼ in / 26 cm

MATERIALS
Yarn:
CYCA #1 (fingering), Tospring (100% wool, 492 yd/450 m / 100 g)
Yarn Color and Amount:
Dark Green 130: 300 g
Needles:
U. S. size 1.5 / 2.5 mm: set of 5 dpn, straight needles, 24 and 32 in / 60 and 80 cm circulars
U.S. size 0 / 2 mm: set of 5 dpn
Gauge:
28 sts and 40 rnds in St st on larger needles = 4 x 4 in / 10 x 10 cm.
Adjust needle sizes to obtain correct gauge if necessary.

CHARTS AND PATTERNS
Edge pattern E-35, page 139
Sleeves—traveling st and star pattern, page 198
Edge pattern E-3, page 135
Vertical panels V-13 and V-14, page 105
Vertical traveling st and star pattern VT-6, page 100.

INSTRUCTIONS

Construction: The sleeves and body are worked from the bottom up. The shoulders are joined with 3-needle BO and then the sleeves are sewn in.

Tip: Make copies of the vertical panel charts and for the vertical traveling st and star patterns that cover the upper body.

SLEEVES (MAKE 2 ALIKE)
Lower edge: With smaller dpn, CO 96 sts using **German twisted CO** method (see page 65). Divide sts evenly onto 4 dpn. Join, being careful not to twist cast-on row; pm for beginning of rnd.
Work 1 **purl braid under** (see page 70).
Next, work 36 rnds of **edge pattern E-35**.

Main pattern: Change to larger dpn and work following instructions and chart for **traveling st and star pattern** as follows:
Rnd 1: Knit, increasing evenly spaced around to 100 sts.
Now divide the sts on dpn as follows:
Needles 1 and 3: 26 sts each.
Needles 2 and 4: 24 sts each.

Rnds 2-74: Begin rnds at the arrow at bottom of chart. On Rnds 35 and 62, rearrange the sts on the needles as indicated by the dark vertical lines:

For example, on Rnd 35:

Needles 1 and 3: 24 sts each;

Needles 2 and 4: 26 sts each.

Rnd 75, Set-up rnd for gusset: Work across Needles 1, 2, and 3 following the chart. Find the center of the star on Needle 1. Count out 28 sts from center, out to both sides for the gusset; pm at each side (the red vertical lines on chart). Work to the last 9 purl sts on Needle 4 up to the first marker.

Now work from chart as follows:

Gusset Row 1 (RS): P1, p2tog, p1, k2, p2, k11, star, k11, p2, k2, p1, p2tog, p1. Place rem sts of rnd onto a holder. Work back and forth on larger (24 in / 60 cm) circular following the chart for the gusset. When charted rows are complete, 3 sts rem.

Next row (WS): Sl 1 knitwise, k1, p1.

Next row (RS): Sl 1 knitwise, k2tog, psso.

Work the second sleeve the same way.

BODY

Lower edge, back: With larger straight needles, CO 140 sts with **German twisted cast-on** (see page 65).

Work 1 **knit braid under** (see page 69).

Next, work **edge pattern E-3** for 2½ in / 6 cm, but begin and end pattern with 4 St sts without edge sts. Last row is on WS; set piece aside.

Lower edge, front: Work as for lower edge, back.

Overlapping join: Work the two lower edges onto larger, longer circular as follows: With RS facing, work across back sts in ribbing to last 4 sts. Hold last 4 sts of back behind first 4 sts of front and join the sets with k2tog (work first st of each needle together). Work across front to last 4 sts and hold them in front of first 4 sts on back. Join the

sets of sts with k2tog = 2 x 136 sts rem.

Pm at center between the 4 joined sts at each side to mark the beginning/end of the back and front pieces. Move markers up on each rnd.

Main pattern: Now work in St st in the round. Increase (M1-loop) 1 st each 6 sts before and after markers (= 4 sts increased per rnd) on every 8th rnd a total of 6 times = 2 x 148 sts. When piece measures 8 in / 20 cm (including lower edge), work charted pattern.

Begin at the marker at right side and work back: *K1, 1 **vertical panel V-13** (7 sts), k2 (St st), **vertical traveling st and star pattern VT-6** (24 sts), k2 (St st), **vertical panel V-14** (7 sts), k62 (St st), **vertical panel V-13** (7 sts), k2 (St st), **vertical traveling st and star pattern VT-6** (24 sts), k2 (St st), **vertical panel V-14** (7 sts), k1 (left side marker)*; rep * to * on front. Work 12 rnds in this main pattern. Divide piece and work front and back separately, back and forth. Place back sts on a holder.

FRONT, CONTINUATION

Working back and forth, continue the pattern as est, but, inc (M1-loop) 1 st at each side. The new sts are edge sts (sl 1 knitwise at beginning of row and p1 at end). When piece measures 14¼ in / 36 cm), begin neckline.

Front neck: Work for 1¼ in / 3 cm in p2, k2 ribbing over the center 50 sts and in St st over the 6 sts between the ribbing and the vertical traveling st and star pattern.

Now, on RS, BO the center 38 sts of ribbing; work to end of row and then work each side separately = 56 sts rem on each side.

Right side: Continue up in pattern (from chart, St st and ribbing), beginning all neck edge rows as: k1, sl 1 knitwise, k1, psso. The outermost st at neck edge is purled on WS so the st remains in St st. Set piece aside when ribbing is eliminated, only 3 of the 6 St sts rem (47 sts rem), and charted rows are completed.

Left side: Work as for right side but work all neck edge rows on WS, decreasing with k2tog inside the St st.

BACK, CONTINUATION

Work as for front, but with 14 more rows before beginning
back neck. Work the back neck as for front. After the
decreases, work straight up in pattern until the second star
has been completed and as much more as necessary for
the sleeves to fit into armhole (steam press—gently under
pressing cloth) and smooth sleeves/armhole before you
measure.

FINISHING

Join shoulders with **3-needle BO** (see page 77). Sew in
sleeves, making sure gussets point downwards.

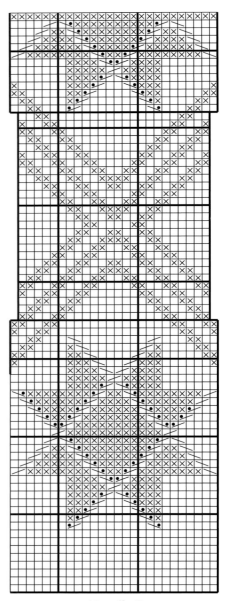

Needle 3

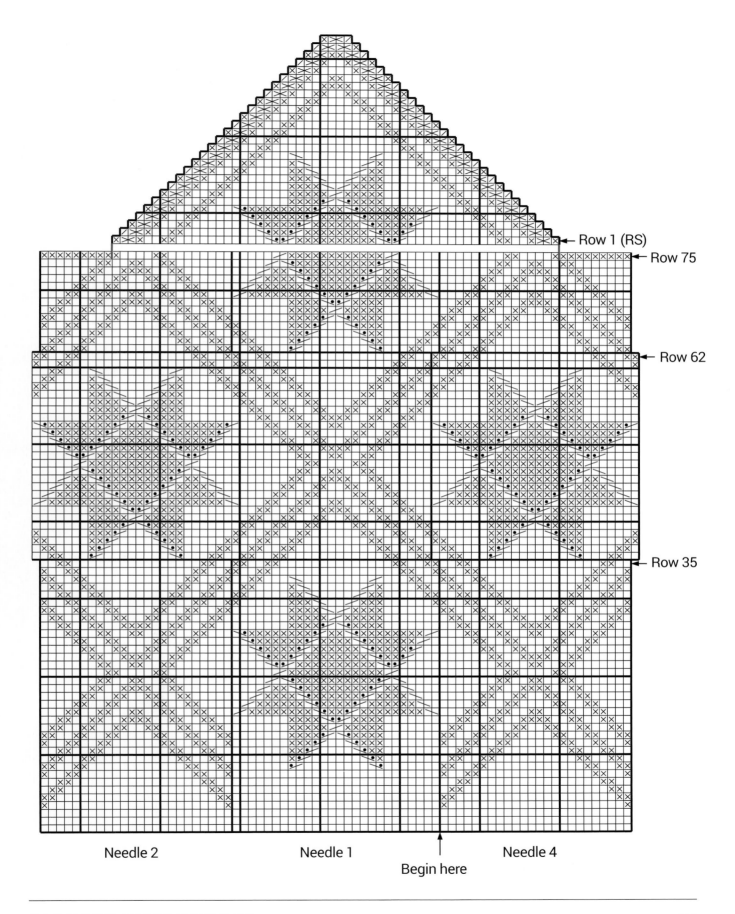

Row 1 (RS)

Row 75

Row 62

Row 35

Needle 2

Needle 1

Needle 4

Begin here

Stole

STOLE

A totally easy stole with traveling stitch and star patterns bordered by an elegant bias-knit band.

SKILL LEVEL
Beginner

FINISHED MEASUREMENTS
Width: 21¾ in / 55 cm
Total Length, Long Side: approx. 86½ in / 220 cm
Total Length, Short Side: approx. 59 in / 150 cm

MATERIALS
Yarn:
CYCA #1 (light fingering), BC Garn Shetlandsuld (Shetland wool) (100% Shetland wool, 492 yd/450 m / 100 g; www.loveknitting.com/us)
Yarn Color and Amount:
White 18: 450 g
Needles:
U. S. size 2.5 / 3 mm: 2 short needles; 32 in / 80 cm circular
Gauge:
24 sts and 42 rows in traveling st and star pattern = 4 x 4 in / 10 x 10 cm.
Adjust needle size to obtain correct gauge if necessary.

CHARTS AND PATTERNS
Traveling st and star pattern, pages 205 and 206

INSTRUCTIONS

Construction: The entire stole is worked from charts. After the body of the stole is complete, a bias-knit band is knitted and sewn on.

STOLE

First triangle: With short straight needles, and using **Knitted CO (K-CO)** method (see page 64), CO 3 sts. Eventually, when sts no longer fit on straight needles, change to circular and work back and forth on it.
Work in **traveling st and star pattern** following instructions below and chart:

Row 1 (RS): K2, p1.
Row 2 (WS): Sl 1 knitwise, p2.
Row 3: K-CO 2 new sts and knit them, k1tbl, p2 = 5 sts.
Row 4: Sl 1 knitwise, p1, k1, p2.
Row 5: K-CO 2 new sts and knit them, k1tbl, p1, k1, p2 = 7 sts.
Row 6: Sl 1 knitwise, p1, k1, p1, k1, p2.
Row 7: K-CO 2 new sts and knit them, k1tbl, p1, k1, p1, k2, p1 = 9 sts.
Row 8: Sl 1 knitwise, p3, k1, p1, k1, p2.
Row 9: K-CO 2 new sts and knit them, k1tbl, p1, k1, p1, k4, p1 = 11 sts.
Row 10: Sl 1 knitwise, p5, k1, p1, k1, p2.

Now continue working from the chart, page 205. Row 11 begins on the right side at the arrow. After completing all charted rows on page 205, go to bottom chart on page 206, beginning at right side at the arrow. At 135 sts, the stole is at its widest.

→

Center section: Continue straight up, working from the same chart with the same edge sts (begin row with with sl 1 knitwise and end with p1). Work pattern repeat across and up until there are 9 stars along the short side and 10 stars along the long side.

Last triangle: End the stole by working from the chart at the top of page 206. Begin all rows on RS with BO 2, always slipping the 1st st at the same time as binding off to make the edging less like stair steps. Continue in pattern until only 3 sts rem; ending on a RS row. Knit 1 row on WS and BO.

BIAS BAND

For the long side: With short straight needles, CO 12 sts and work as follows:

Row 1 (WS): Purl across.

Row 2: Sl 1 knitwise, M1-loop (see page 67), knit until 3 sts rem, end k2tog, p1.

Row 3: Sl 1 knitwise, purl across.

Repeat Rows 2-3 until band measures approx. 102¼ in / 260 cm. Set aside.

For the short side and the diagonal sides: Make 1 band approx. 124 in / 315 cm long.

FINISHING

First sew the shortest band securely to stole (as invisibly and elastically as possible) along the long side inside the edge st on the side of the band where the M1-loop increases are. The band should not make the stole ruffle, but it shouldn't draw it in either. You need to be a little deft (the first time I tried this, I sewed down one side and then saw that I needed to undo it and try again!). Fold the band in half and sew down on WS. About 8 in / 20 cm of the band should hang off the end on each of the 2 points.

Working the same way, sew the band along the two diagonal sections and the short straight side, also leaving about 8 in / 20 cm hanging off the ends. The corners will take a bit of extra finessing but it will be worth the effort. Make a knot with the 2 band ends at each corner (see photo, page 202).

WHOLE STOLE

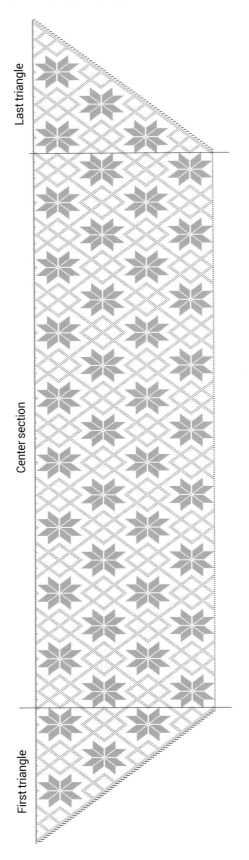

Last triangle

Center section

First triangle

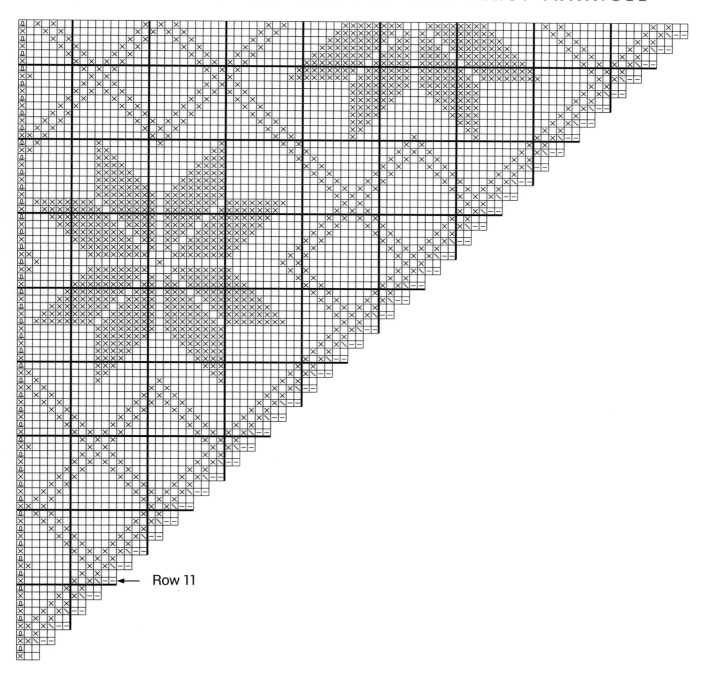

Row 11

TRAVELING STITCH AND STAR PATTERN—LAST TRIANGLE

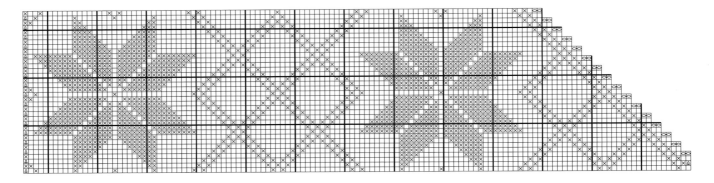

TRAVELING STITCH AND STAR PATTERN—FIRST TRIANGLE (CONTINUATION) AND CENTER SECTION

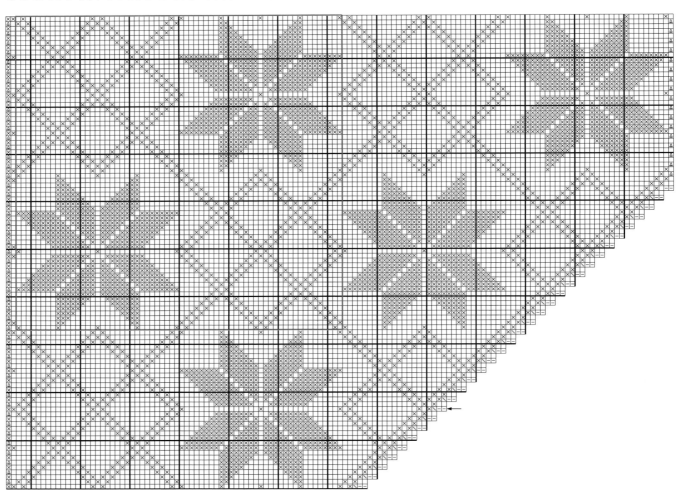

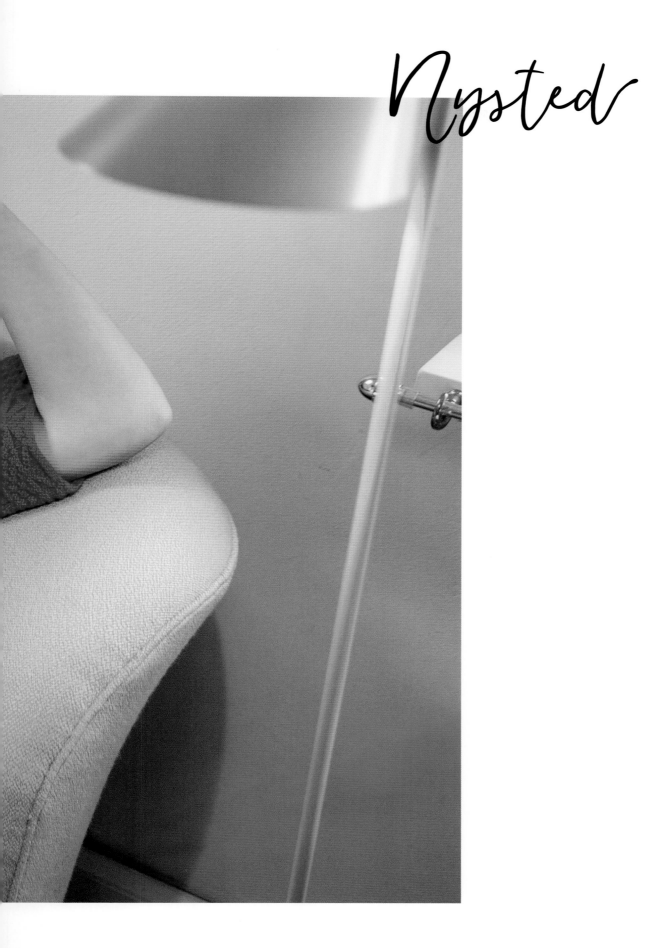

Nysted

NYSTED SWEATER

This sweater was modeled on a fine sweater from Nysted on Lolland. Lolland sweaters typically have horizontal panels and traveling stitch and star patterns as all-over designs on the body and sleeves. The women who produced the original sweaters knitted a braid after the cast-on row to reinforce the edge and add embellishment. The sweater is further embellished with a beautiful silk ribbon sewn around the neck.

SKILL LEVEL
Intermediate

FINISHED MEASUREMENTS
Circumference: 41¾ in / 106 cm
Total Length: 21¾ in / 55 cm
Sleeve Length: 9¾ in / 25 cm

MATERIALS
Yarn: CYCA #1 (fingering), Trekant (Triangle) (100% wool, 492 yd/450 m / 100 g)
Yarn Color and Amount:
Red 10: 400-500 g (the sweater in the photo weighs precisely 400 g)
Notions: Silk ribbon band, 2½ in / 6 cm wide and approx. 25½ in / 65 cm long (available from www.silke-annet.dk)
Needles:
U. S. size 1.5 / 2.5 mm: set of 5 dpn; straight needles; 32 in / 80 cm circular
Gauge:
28 sts and 47 rows in traveling st and star pattern = 4 x 4 in / 10 x 10 cm.
Adjust needle size to obtain correct gauge if necessary.

CHARTS AND PATTERNS
Horizontal Panel H-12, page 95
Sleeves and body—horizontal panels and traveling st and star pattern, page 214
Edge pattern E-9, page 135

INSTRUCTIONS

Construction: The sleeves and body are worked from the bottom up. The shoulders are joined with **3-needle BO**. The sleeves are sewn in and then the silk ribbon is sewn around the neck.

SLEEVES (MAKE 2 ALIKE)

Lower edge: With dpn, CO 96 sts using **German twisted cast-on** (see page 65). Be sure you add enough extra length for the braid. Divide sts evenly onto 4 dpn and join, being careful not to twist cast-on row. Pm for beginning of rnd.

Work 30 rnds for the sleeve edge following the chart for **horizontal panel H-12**. Work the repeat (framed in red) a total of 8 times each rnd. All the braids are purl, over. Afterwards, begin each rnd with p1 as a "seam" st.

Main pattern: Continue in traveling st and star pattern (framed in green). Increase 1 st each before and after the sleeve "seam" (p1) on every 4th rnd a total of 14 times and then on every other rnd 14 times = 152 sts. BO loosely.

BODY

Lower edge, body: With straight needles, CO 144 sts with **German twisted cast-on** (page 65). Don't forget to add enough extra length for the braid.
Work 1 **knit braid under** (see page 69).
Now work 28 rnds in **edge pattern E-9** without edge sts—all the sts are worked in pattern.
Set piece aside.

Lower edge, back: Work as for front lower edge.

Joining edges without overlapping or cable twist (RS): Use an extra ball of yarn for the braid or pull the yarn from both the inside and outside of the ball. Work the two edges onto the circular, *at the same time* as working the purl braid, under (see page 70). Next, knit 1 rnd, increasing 3 sts evenly spaced on both front and back = 2 x 147 sts.

Panel:
Work the **horizontal panel** following the chart (bottom 17 rows on chart):
Rnd 1: Work along the back: k10, *p2, k11, p1, k11*; rep * to * until 12 sts rem, end p2, k10. Work across the front the same way.
Rnds 2-16: Continue following chart, working the decreases at the sides as indicated.
Rnd 17: 1 **purl braid under** (page 70).

Main pattern:
Rnd 21: K2, pm (for beginning of rnd to the armhole and to set off the gusset and body, p1, work 125 sts in **traveling st and star pattern**, p1, k4 (gusset), p1, 125 sts in **traveling st and star pattern**, p1, k4 (gusset). There are now 127 sts between the gussets on, respectively, the back and front.

Work the large **traveling st and star pattern** (repeat is framed in red) and, *at the same time*, increase for the gussets on each side as shown on the chart on every 6th rnd. Continue up, repeating the pattern framed in red for the traveling st and star pattern and gussets until piece measures approx. 11½ in / 29 cm. Divide the work into 2 equal pieces at the center of each gusset for the armholes. The back and front are now worked separately.

FRONT, CONTINUATION

Continue in charted **traveling st and star pattern** and gussets until piece measures approx. 18¼ in / 46 cm. On a RS row, BO the center 35 sts and work each side separately.
Right side: Begin all rows at neck edge on RS with k1, sl 1 knitwise, k1, psso a total of 7 times. Do not decrease on WS rows but always knit the last st.
After completing decreases, work straight up until the neckline depth is 4 in / 10 cm. End with a ridge on RS (= knit 1 row on WS or purl on RS). This finishes the front; set piece aside.
Left side: Work the last 3 sts on all RS rows/at neck edge as: k2tog, k1. Do not decrease on WS but always knit the first st. Continue as for right side.

BACK, CONTINUATION

Work straight up until piece measures approx. 21¼ in / 54 cm. On a RS row, BO the center 45 sts and then work each side separately.
Right side: Work as for left side of front, decreasing only 2 times.
The last row is on WS (no ridge on RS).
Left side: Work as for right side of front, decreasing only 2 times.

FINISHING

Join the shoulders with **3-needle BO** (see page 77). Sew sleeves into armholes. Sew the silk ribbon along the neck (if desired, only on the front neck).

⟶

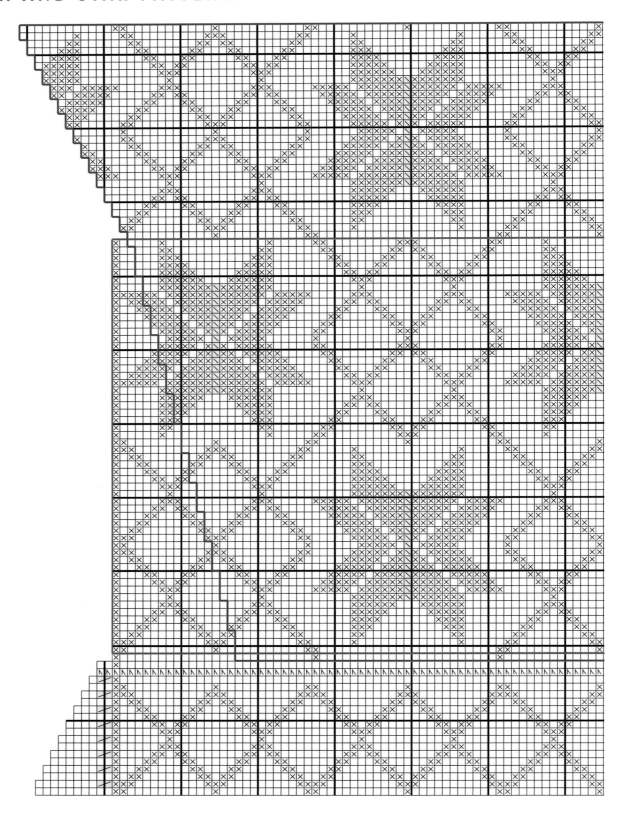

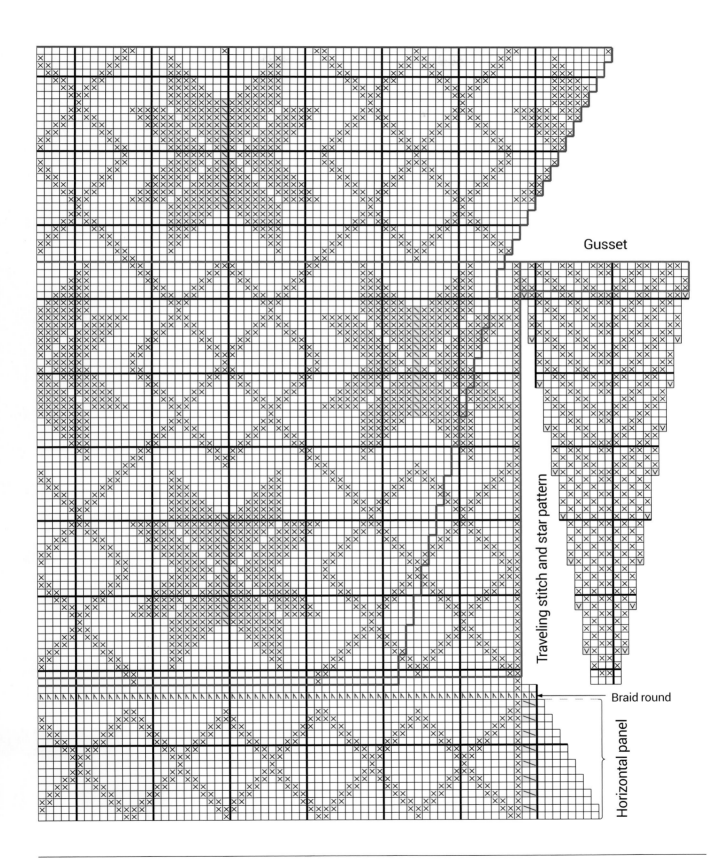

Gusset

Traveling stitch and star pattern

Braid round

Horizontal panel

Top

TOP

A lovely and practical little top or vest. The center of each star is decorated with beads.

SKILL LEVEL
Intermediate

FINISHED MEASUREMENTS
Circumference: 41¾ in / 106 cm
Total Length: 21 in / 53 cm

MATERIALS
Yarn:
CYCA #3 (DK, light worsted), Rowan Wool
Cotton (50% cotton, 50% Merino wool, 124
yd/113 m / 50 g; www.knitrowan.com)
Yarn Color and Amount:
Flower (mocha) 943: 8 balls
Optional Notions: Glass beads; sewing or
beading needle and thread to match sweater yarn (make sure needle goes through
chosen beads)
Needles: U. S. size 2.5 / 3 mm: straight
needles; 32 in / 80 cm circular; set of 3 dpn
Crochet Hook: U. S. D-3 / 3 mm
Gauge:
24 sts and 35 rnds in traveling st and star
pattern = 4 x 4 in / 10 x 10 cm.
Adjust needle size to obtain correct gauge
if necessary.

CHARTS AND PATTERNS
Edge pattern E-22, page 137
Body—horizontal panel, page 221
Body—traveling st and star pattern, page
222

INSTRUCTIONS

Construction: The body is worked from the bottom up. The shoulders are joined with **3-needle BO** and then the sleeves are sewn in. Beads can be added as decoration.

BODY

Lower edge, back: With straight needles, CO 126 sts with **long-tail cast-on.** Knit 10 rows (no edge sts—all knit), ending with a RS row.

Now work 20 rows **edge pattern E-22** with 4 knit sts at each side (all the way up). Begin as follows:
Row 1 (WS): K4, (p4, k2) to last 8 sts, end p4, k4.
Row 2 (RS): K4, (k4, p2) to last 8 sts, end k8.

Rep Rows 1-2 9 more times, ending on WS, *and*, on last row, increasing 1 st inside the first 4 sts (= 127 sts or 119 sts + 4 edge sts on each side).

Horizontal panel: Knit 2 rows = 1 ridge on RS.
Now work the **horizontal panel** following the chart and this set-up: K4 (edge sts not included on chart), work from A to B (6 sts), from B to C (9 times = 108 sts), and C to D (5 sts); end with k4 (edge sts not included on chart). Work 8 rows on chart and, *at the same time*, continue the k4 edge sts up on each side. End with k2 rows and set piece aside.

Lower edge, front: Work as for back lower edge.

→

Joining with overlap: Join the two edges on a circular as follows on RS: Knit front edge until 4 sts rem. Hold first 4 sts of back behind last 4 sts of front. Knit the 2 sets of sts tog (join 1st st on front with 1st st of back needle). Knit across back to last 4 sts. Hold the last 4 sts of back behind the first 4 sts of front and join as before. Now begin working in the round.

Main pattern: Work in **traveling st and star pattern—body** over the center 119 sts (the entire chart) on both back and front, continuing the 4 garter sts at each side as the "seam." Garter sts in the round = alternate knit and purl rnds.

Work the repeat framed in red, *but*, on the second rep, divide the piece at Underarm on chart in the center of the 4 garter sts at each side. Set piece aside.

FRONT, CONTINUATION

K-CO 2 new sts (page 64), at the beginning and end of the first row. Continue in pattern, working back and forth, with the 4 outermost sts in garter st. At Front neck on the chart, end on WS and continue as below:

Next Row (RS): Work until 3 sts before the center st (red block), p2tog, k1, place the center st on a safety pin or waste yarn, k1, p2tog, continue from chart to end of row. Now work each side separately.

Right side:

Next Row (WS): Work until 2 sts before center st, k2tog, k1.
Next Row (RS): P1, p2tog, k2 and continue in pattern, end k4.
Next Row (WS): K4, pattern to last 3 sts, k2tog, k1.
Rep the last 2 rows until 41 sts rem. Now work without decreasing, with 2 reverse St sts (= purl on RS and knit on WS) inside garter edge sts at side to shoulder.
Set piece aside.

Left side: Work to correspond to right side, beginning at the center.
Next Row (WS): K1, k2tog, k1 and continue in pattern, ending with k4.
Next Row (RS): Work to last 4 sts, p1, p2tog, p1.
Rep these 2 rows until 41 sts rem.
Continue in pattern without decreasing with 2 reverse St sts inside edge sts which continue in garter st. Set piece aside when at shoulder.

BACK, CONTINUATION

Work back as for front but begin the neck shaping at BN (back neck) on chart. BO the center 37 sts on RS and work each side separately.

Left side: Work 1 row on WS and, on next row, BO 4 sts at neck edge. Work 4 more rows. Place sts on a dpn and set piece aside.

Right side: Begin at side and work 1 row on RS. On next row, BO 4 sts at neck edge. Work 4 more rows. Place sts on a dpn and set piece aside.

FINISHING

Join shoulders with **3-needle BO** (page 77).
Crochet in **crab st** around the neck (page 249). If desired, sew 4 beads at center of each star over the St st.

BODY—HORIZONTAL PANEL

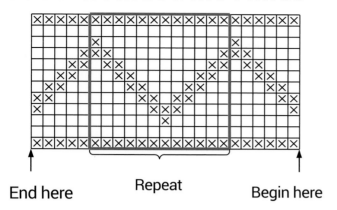

End here   Repeat   Begin here

Split edge and overlapped join.
Note the side "seam" above the join.

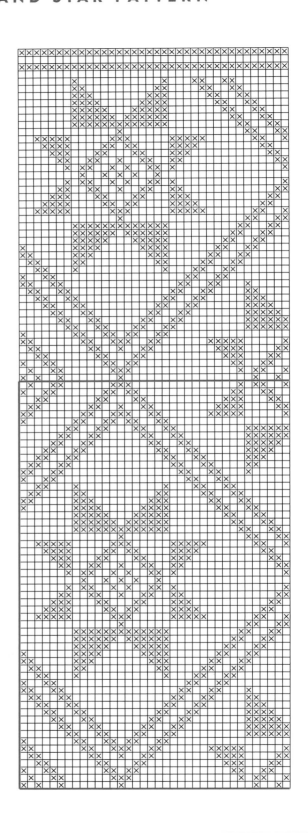

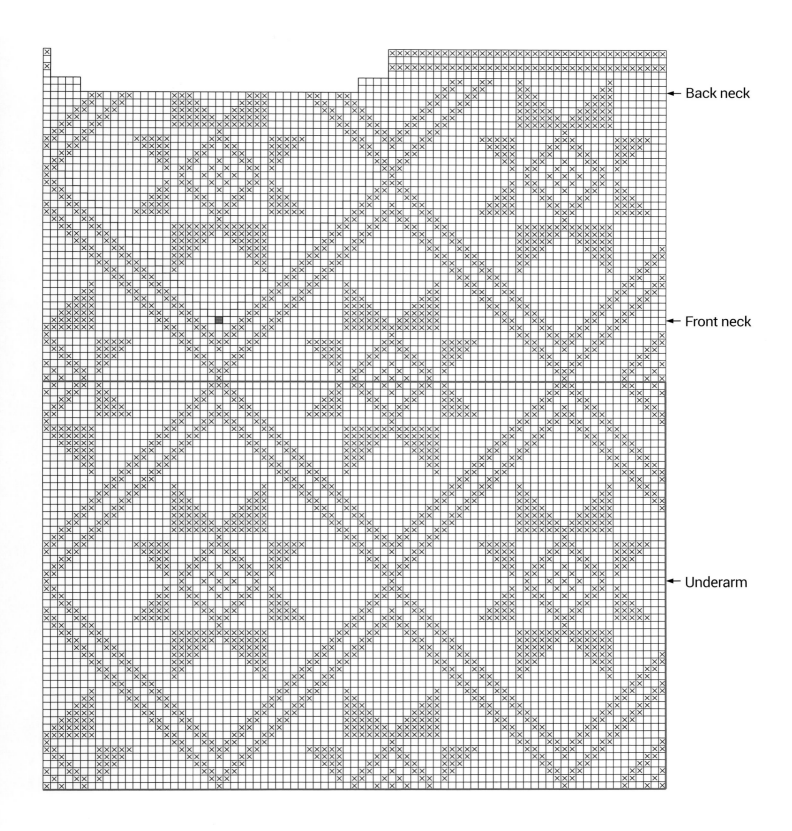

← Back neck

← Front neck

← Underarm

Kirsten

KIRSTEN'S SWEATER

Patterned edges, horizontal panels, and the main pattern on this pullover are each worked in their own shade of red. The horizontal panel pattern is repeated on the outside of the neckband with the edge pattern making an encore on the inside. The sweater is designed with positive ease hence the raised edge. See page 235 for an explanation of how the number of stitches, needle size, and increases were calculated.

SKILL LEVEL
Intermediate

FINISHED MEASUREMENTS
Circumference: 45¾ in / 116 cm
Total Length: 23¾ in / 60 cm
Sleeve Length: 17¼ in / 44 cm
To calculate measurements, see page 235

MATERIALS
Yarn:
(CYCA #1, light fingering), Blackhill CottonWool (50% cotton, 50% Merino wool, 252 yd/230 m / 50 g)
Yarn Colors and Amounts:
Color A: Blood Orange 98: 6 balls
Color B: Deep Red 91: 2 balls
Color C: Raspberry Sorbet 80: 1 ball
Needles:
U. S. size 1.5 / 2.5 mm: set of 5 dpn; straight needles; 24 and 32 in / 60 and 80 cm circulars; 16 in / 40 cm circular (optional)
U.S. size 0 / 2 mm: set of 5 dpn
Gauge:
28 sts and 44 rnds in traveling st and star pattern = 4 x 4 in / 10 x 10 cm.
Adjust needle sizes to obtain correct gauge if necessary.

CHARTS AND PATTERNS
Edge pattern E-14, page 136
Sleeves—horizontal panel, page 229
Sleeves—traveling st and star pattern, page 230
Body—horizontal panel, page 229
Body—traveling st and star pattern, page 229

INSTRUCTIONS

Construction: The sleeves and body are worked from the bottom up. The shoulders are joined with 3-needle BO and then the sleeves are sewn in. The neckband is worked last.

SLEEVES (MAKE 2 ALIKE)
Lower edge: With Color B and U. S. size 0 / 2 mm dpn, CO 68 sts with **long-tail cast-on**. Divide sts evenly onto 4 dpn. Join, being careful not to twist cast-on row; pm for beginning of rnd. Work **edge pattern E-14** for 2½ in / 6 cm, ending with Row 2 or 4 of chart.
Change to Color C and knit 1 rnd, *at the same time*, increasing 8 sts evenly spaced around = 76 sts.

Horizontal panel: Change to U. S. size 1.5 / 2.5 mm dpn and work 11 rnds **horizontal panel** following the chart: Work from A to B (22 sts), from B to C 5 times (50 sts), and from C to D (4 sts). On the 10th rnd, increase 1 st (M1-loop) at the top of each chevron at the green lines on the chart = 83 sts.
Change to Color A and knit 1 rnd, increasing 9 sts evenly spaced around = 92 sts.

Main pattern: Divide the sts with 23 on each of the 4 dpn. Work in **traveling st and star pattern**. On the last rnd of the 2nd pattern tier and then on last rnd of every pattern rep, increase with M-1 loop at the red lines on chart a total of 4 times. BO loosely when sleeve is desired length.

BODY
Lower edge, back: With Color B and U. S. size 1.5 / 2.5 mm straights, CO 162 sts with **long-tail cast-on**. Knit 1 row (WS).

Next, work in **edge pattern E-14** without edge sts (work all sts across in pattern) for 3¼ in / 8 cm. End with either Row 2 or 4 of chart (WS). Set piece aside.

Lower edge, front: Work as for back lower edge.

Overlapping Join: Work the two edges onto 32 in / 80 cm circular U. S. size 1.5 / 2.5 mm as follows, beginning on RS with Color C: Knit across back, *at the same time* increasing 5 sts evenly spaced across, until 2 sts rem. Hold last 2 sts of back behind first 2 sts of front and join the sets of sts with k2tog (join the first st on each needle). Knit across front, *at the same time* increasing 5 sts evenly spaced across, until 2 sts rem. Hold first 2 sts of back behind last 2 sts of front and join as before, ending with sl 1 purlwise with yarn in back = 330 sts. Now begin working in the round.

Horizontal panel: Work 11 rnds of the **horizontal panel** from A to B (11 sts), and then B to C 15 times (150 sts), k4 (side seam), rep horizontal panel on back and end with k4 side seam (rep seam sts all the way up).

Main pattern: Change to Color A and knit 1 rnd (except for side seams which continue as est).
Now work in charted **traveling st and star pattern** over the 161 sts each of front and back as follows:
Begin at A and work to B (23) sts, from B to C (46 sts) 3 times—then work the 4 side seam sts. After 45 rnds rep the pattern (44 rnds) until the piece measures 15 in / 38 cm (10¾ in / 27.5 cm) from the horizontal panel. Divide the piece in the center of each 4-st side seam and then work each side separately back and forth. Begin and end the first row (RS) on both back and front by casting on 3 sts at each side (K-CO suggested) so that the side seams continue up with 1 edge st (knit on all rows) at each side.

FRONT, CONTINUATION

After completing 4 rep (176 rows) traveling st and star pattern, BO the center 17 sts on RS and then work each side separately.

Right side: To round neck, BO 2 sts at the beginning of each RS row 8 times. Then work straight up for another 16-17 rows, after completing center of a star. Set piece aside.

Left side: Work to correspond to right side, binding off on WS rows.

BACK, CONTINUATION

After working 27 more rnds/rows of traveling st and star pattern than front's 176 rnds/rows, BO the center 37 sts and work each side separately.

Right side: For back neck, BO 4-2 sts at beginning of next two WS rows. Continue straight up and put piece aside when at same length as front.

Left side: Work as for right side, binding off on RS rows.

FINISHING

Join shoulders with **3-needle BO** (see page 77).

NECKBAND

With shorter circular U. S. size 1.5 / 2.5 mm and Color C, pick up and knit sts around neck: 39 sts at side neck (from back neck to front neck), 17 sts at base of front neck, 39 sts from front to back neck, and 58 sts along back neck = 154 sts total.

Neckband: Work 11 rnds **horizontal panel—body**, omitting the 4 side seam sts. On rnd 2, decrease 4 sts evenly spaced across back neck. Begin the chevron pattern at A on chart. On the next-to-last rnd, k2tog centered between each point.

Neckband lining: Change to Color B and knit 1 rnd. Work 8 rnds **edge pattern**, and *at the same time*, on 1st rnd, increase 1 st. BO loosely; fold band in half and sew down edge on WS.

Sew in sleeves.

SLEEVES—HORIZONTAL PANEL   BODY—HORIZONTAL PANEL

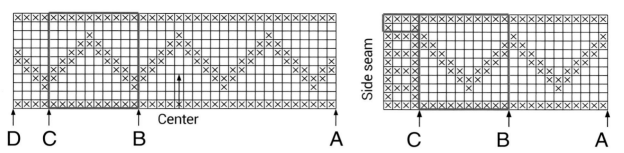

BODY—TRAVELING STITCH AND STAR PATTERN

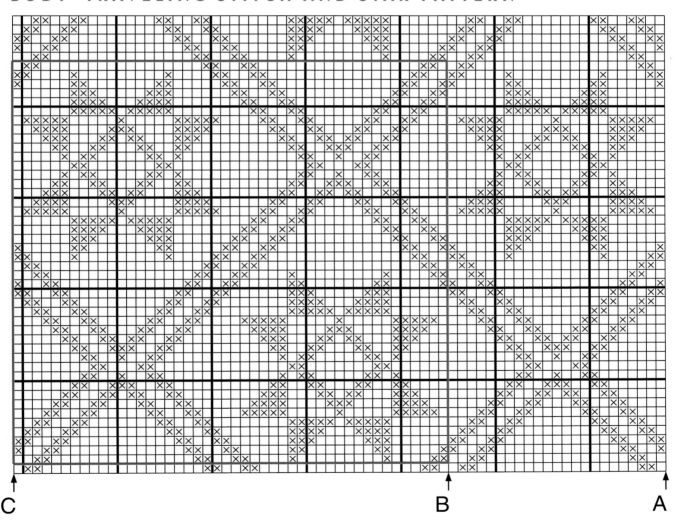

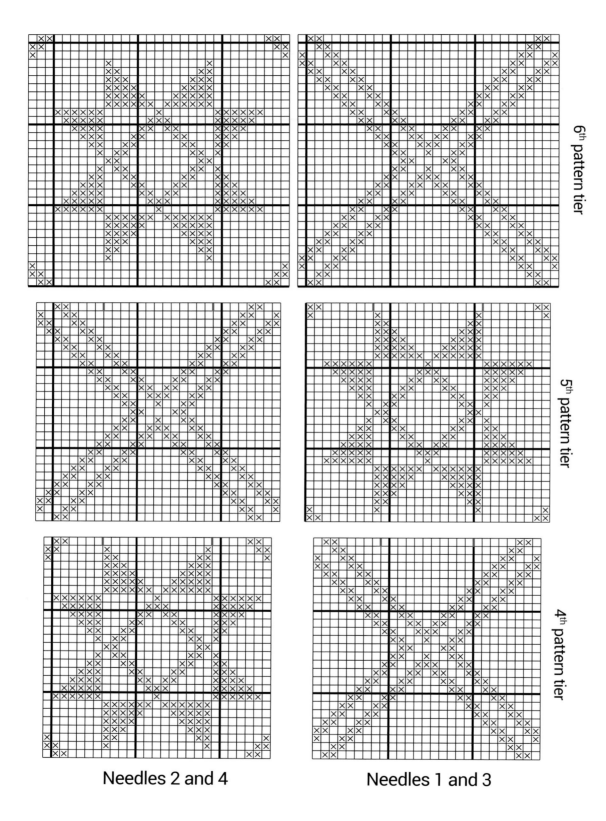

6th pattern tier

5th pattern tier

4th pattern tier

Needles 2 and 4

Needles 1 and 3

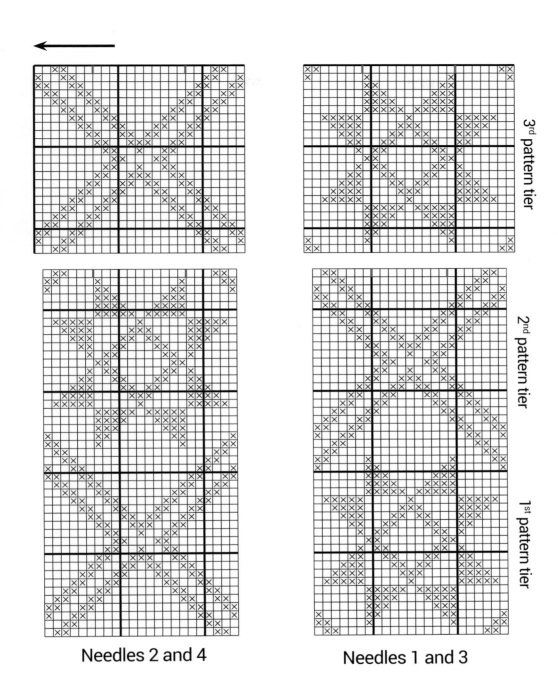

3rd pattern tier

2nd pattern tier

1st pattern tier

Needles 2 and 4

Needles 1 and 3

YOUR OWN
NIGHT SWEATER

KNIT YOUR OWN NIGHT SWEATER

This is not a specific pattern but rather a collection of advice and suggestions for anyone wanting to design a night sweater using the many motifs in this book. The garment preparation includes 5 steps, starting with: an overview, how the sweater should look, and knitting a gauge swatch. Then you calculate the stitch and row/round counts and the rate of increase. Draw a sketch of the sweater and arrange the patterns as you like. Now you are ready to knit!

PREPARATION

1. Sizing the sweater
Find a sweater in a size and style similar to the one you want to knit and take all the measurements from this. In the example given here, the measurements are taken from Kirsten's Sweater. See also the schematic on the facing page.

2. Models, ideas, thoughts
Look over the old and new sweaters in this book and select a few designs. Think about what you want your sweater to look like. Should it simply copy the old sweaters, or do you want to adapt the patterns in a totally untraditional way? Draw one or more sketches.

3. Patterns
Choose the motifs for your sweater.

4. Yarn
Choose yarn and needles that match for the fabric you want. In the example, we used U. S. size 1.5 / 2.5 mm.

5. Gauge
Determine your gauge by knitting a swatch in the motif you want to use for the main pattern—that is, the most extensive pattern.
CO 40 sts on needles U. S. size 1.5 / 2.5 mm, for example, and knit in pattern for 6 in / 15 cm. Measure a section of the swatch 4 x 4 in / 10 x 10 cm, counting the number of stitches and rows.
Using Kirsten's Sweater as an example:
28 sts and 44 rows = 4 x 4 in / 10 x 10 cm.
Dividing the count by 4 for inches, we get **7 sts and 11 rows per inch**, or, for centimeters, divide by 10 and we have **2.8 sts and 4.4 rows per cm.**

MEASUREMENTS FOR KIRSTEN'S SWEATER

Sleeve width, top (ST): 17¼ in / 44 cm

Sleeve width, above lower edge: 10¾ in / 27 cm

Sleeve width above horizontal panel (SaE) 12¾ in / 32 cm

Sleeve length (SL): 17¼ in / 44 cm

Chest width (half circumference; ½ C): 22¾ in / 58 cm

Total length (TL): 23¾ in / 60 cm

CALCULATIONS

Do not omit measuring and counting before you knit. See the information below.

SLEEVES WITH SEAMS

The following example shows you how to count the number of stitches and rows for sleeves to be worked **back and forth** on two needles, from the bottom up. As you work, increases are worked along the underarm which will become a sort of seam. Finally, the sleeves are sewn together.

Sleeve, lower edge

Usually people prefer the lower edge or cuff of a sleeve to be somewhat snug around the wrist. So, you should count on fewer stitches than above the cuff and, if included, a horizontal panel (SE = sleeve edge). Normally, the cuff is

worked straight up in an elastic pattern, so we have not included the width of the lower sleeves on the schematic.

Horizontal panel

Above the sleeve edge or cuff, night sweaters typically have a horizontal panel. Usually the stitch count needs to be adjusted so the stitch count above the edge fits the count needed for the panel. You might also need to adjust the count by increasing above the horizontal panel so it fits the count for the main pattern on the sleeve.

Calculating the stitch count above the lower edge (and, if included, the horizontal panel):
Multiply the SE measurement by the number of sts per in / cm (7 sts / 2.8 sts):
12¾ in x 7 sts = 89.25, rounded up to 90 sts / 32 cm x 2.8 sts = 89.6 sts, rounded up to 90 sts.

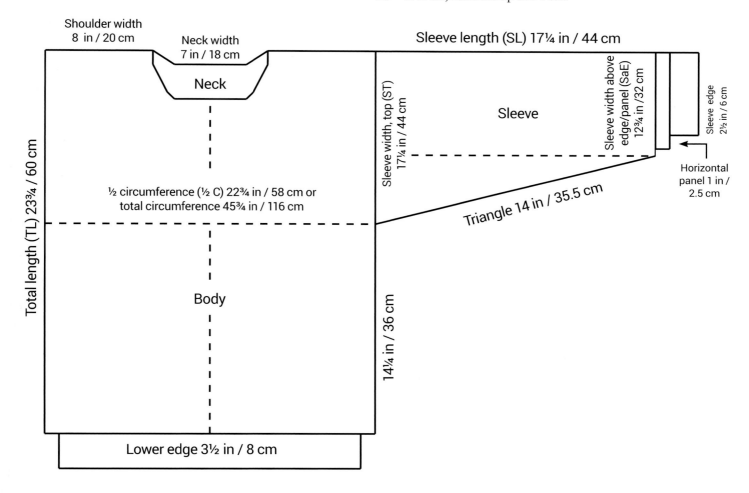

Calculating the stitch count at underarm

Multiply the ST measurement by the number of sts per in / cm:

17¼ in x 7 = 120.75
44 cm x 2.8 sts = 123.2 sts.
Round up to 124 sts.

Calculating the number of rows

Multiply the SL measurement—the edge (2½ in / 6 cm) and, if applicable, horizontal panel by the number of rows per in / cm:

11 rows = 1 in / 2.5 cm:
17¼—3¼ in = 14 in / 44 cm—8.5 cm / 35.5 cm.

Multiply SL by the number of rows per in / cm:
14 in x 11 rows = 154 rows.
35.5 cm x 4.4 rows = 156.2 rows.
Round up to 156 rows.

Calculating the number of increases

Subtract the SaB from the ST:
124 sts—90 sts = 34 sts.

Divide the result by 2 since you will increase 1 st at each side of sleeve "seam".
34 sts / 2 = 17 sts.
This gives the number of sts to be increased on each side, spaced over 156 rows.

Calculating the spacing of increase rows.

Divide the number of rows with the number of increases:
156 / 17 = 9.176.
Of course, you can't space the increases every 9.176 rows, so you need to even out the spacing. In this case, the increases can be staggered on every 8th and 10th row, so all increases will be on the RS. Read the following for more information about increase intervals.

Calculating on graph paper

The equation doesn't always work out, so I suggest doing some of the work by hand by using graph paper (preferably with small squares)—see the "Triangle" chart.
Draw a frame as for the green one on the chart on the next page and also take a look at the "Triangle" on the schematic on page 235:
17 blocks in width x 156 blocks in length = 17 sts x 156 rows.

Draw a diagonal line from corner to corner (red line on the chart). Now you can add "stairs" to represent the increases. Begin at the bottom with 1 increase every 10th row. Also mark the increases by working down from the top with an increase every 8th row. See if the lines meet or if they need to be adjusted. When knitting back and forth, it is best with an even row count (increase every 8th and 10th row on RS rows.

The increase instructions will be stated in a pattern as:
Increase 1 st each at the beginning and end of every 10th row 6 times and every 8th row 11 times.

A SEAMLESS NIGHT SWEATER

Here are some details if you are knitting the sleeves in the round from the bottom up, without seams, on 4 dpn, with a 5th to knit with.

Calculations: Measure, calculate the stitch count, number of rows, and increases for the sleeve as for working back and forth. If the increases are still different, see below under main pattern.

Sleeve edge: The sleeve edges should have somewhat fewer stitches than the SaE. See "Sleeves with seams."

Horizontal panel: See "Sleeves with seams."

Main pattern: Even here the stitch count must be adjusted somewhat. **Note:** For each main pattern with traveling stitches and stars on pages 116-133, the repeat is indicated and the center marked with a dotted line. This shows where the pattern can be divided for the sleeves so that one half of a repeat (for example, a star) can be placed on one dpn, the second (a traveling stitch motif, for example) on the next needle; the sts are divided the same way on Needles 3 and 4.
As you work around and up the sleeve, increase 8 sts after every complete star (= 2 sts increased per dpn). This will enlarge the traveling stitch motifs and stars as you work up the sleeve. Or you can simply use the charts for Kirsten's Sweater on page 224 or the Frenderup Sweater on page 164.

If you are adding a gusset at the underarm, you'll need to include that in your calculation. Or you can work straight up until sleeve is desired length.

BODY

Calculating the stitch count above the lower edge

Multiply ½ C with the number of sts per in / cm:
22¾ in x 7 sts = 159.25 / 58 cm x 2.8 sts = 162.4 sts.
Round up / down to an even number: 162 sts.

Calculating the stitch count for lower edge

Usually it is preferable for the lower edge to draw in a bit,
as for example, on a ribbed edge (E-1 to E-5). In that case,
start with about 10% fewer stitches. Kirsten's Sweater
doesn't have a tighter edge, so she used all 162 sts.

Neckline width and depth

For the neck width and depth, use the measurements
from your model sweater. An old rule of thumb is that
the neck should be approximately one-third of ½ C which
also depends on the body width and shaping. If you are
making a sweater with inset sleeves as for Kirsten's, this
won't be completely off base. The neckline depth is 2½-4
in / 6-10 cm for a typical rounded neck but this can also
vary. Finally, the width of the neck edge also influences the
width and depth of the neckline.

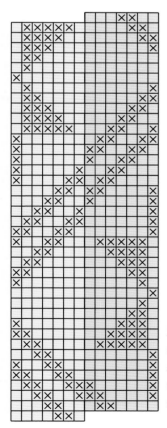

NOTE: When knitting in the round, you are making a spiral so the motifs will not meet precisely from round to round.

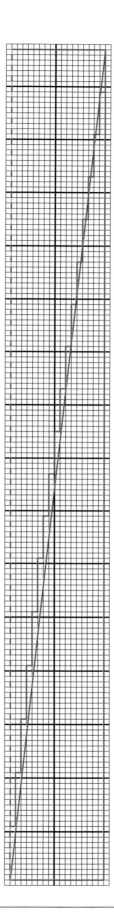

TRIANGLE

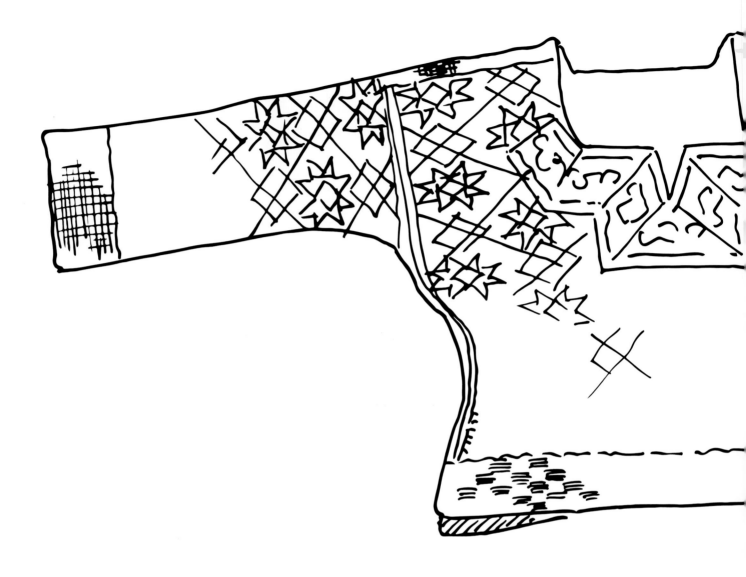

ARRANGING THE PATTERN MOTIFS

CHOOSING THE MOTIFS

Find the patterns you would like to use from pages 78-139.

For the sleeves: Sleeves are typically covered with an edge pattern, possibly a horizontal panel, and a main overall pattern. Of course, you can choose to add one or more vertical panels to run up the sleeve from the edge or something completely different.

Some patterns are so large that you can't fit two repeats around, and in that case you have to adjust the pattern. Draw a smaller version of the design on graph paper—it's relatively easy to do. See "Anatomy of Knitted Stars" on the next page.

For the body: You can begin with an edge pattern and, if desired, a horizontal panel. Choose a main pattern to place above the lower edge, for example, vertical panels or stars stacked over each other as for Annie's Sweater (shown on page 174) or spread randomly over the front. There are so many options.

PATTERN PLACEMENT

Decide on the pattern arrangement and work from the center out.

Lower edge: Once you've decided which patterns to use, you have to do some calculations. Kirsten used E-14, which is a multiple of 4 + 2. The stitch count on the sleeves can be a multiple of 4 but, on the body, which is worked back and forth, you want to make sure the pattern is positioned symmetrically on both sides of the split sides. So, subtract 2 sts from 162 sts = 160 sts; the number must be a multiple of 4 and, luckily, in this case it is. If you want an edge stitch at each side, you need to add 2 sts, so the total to cast on is 164 sts.

If you are going to join the lower edges at the sides with an overlap, you need to take that into account as the stitch count above the edge becomes smaller. If you are joining the edges with a cable twist, the stitch count remains unchanged.

Horizontal panel: For a horizontal panel above the lower edge, the stitch count might need to be adjusted before the panel begins. If you are adding side patterns, calculate the numbers for them—the same rules apply as for the lower edge.

Main section of body: Place the main pattern(s) above the edge and horizontal panel. Kirsten chose an overall traveling stitch and star pattern while Annie positioned stars at the center and in vertical panels out towards the sides. Both Kirsten's and Annie's sweaters have side seams. No matter what you choose, you will need to determine whether you need an even or odd number of stitches. This is, in turn, determined by the center of the pattern at the center of the piece so you can count out to the sides for the correct pattern placement.

Neckband: Finally, you have to decide on the style of neckband you prefer. Annie only knitted an edge below the bind-off while Kirsten's Sweater has a round neck with a folded edge.

KNITTING TIPS FOR GOOD FIT

I think that at the height of night sweater knitting, one first knitted the sleeves and put them aside without binding off. The body was worked next with the shoulder stitches left on holders. Finally, the sweater is tried on (with the body and separate sleeves). If the sleeves were too short, they could be lengthened, and if the armhole was not deep enough, the back shoulders could be lengthened. I recommend that today's night sweater knitters follow the same procedure. This hasn't been written down in any instructions but note that the patterns here begin with the sleeves.

TIPS FOR USING THE PATTERNS

ANATOMY OF KNITTED STARS

When knitting, it is logical that stars should be symmetrical and made with 8 points: 2 pointing down, 2 pointing up, and 2 on each side. This way, the star will be constructed with the same number of stitches across as rows in height. If, for example, the points which turn outwards respectively to the right and left consist of 6 sts/6 rows, then the points up and down should also have 6 sts and 6 rows. In most case, there's also 1 st between the vertical points. You can calculate a star as:

(6 + 6) + 1 + (6 + 6) sts/rows = 25 sts/25 rows.

Following the same logic, you can alter star sizes, so 2 stitches added in width means 2 more rows are needed in height.

Another option for variation is to change the pattern structure (in knit and purl) to a multicolored pattern. In Norwegian patterns, we see stars (also called "8-petal roses") knitted with several colors—you can also do this with "our" stars. See, for example, the tunic on page 158.

REPEATS AND STARS

Stars do not appear as pattern repeats, but of course stars can be repeated and even arranged "randomly" on a body. Within the traveling stitch and star motifs, you can also substitute other star patterns. Just check to see whether the netting of the traveling stitch pattern has an even or odd number of stitches. If it is an odd number, find a star with an uneven stitch count, and if it is even, choose a star motif with an even stitch count.

SLEEVES AND INCREASES

My best recommendation is that you begin the sleeves with an edge pattern. You can figure out the stitch count from other sweaters. The stitch count should be evenly divisible over 4 double-pointed needles, with the fifth used to knit with. When the edge is complete, you will likely need to increase somewhat and then begin with the bottom points of the star tips (or with the top half of a star) on 2 needles and the traveling stitch (or the top half of a traveling stitch pattern on the other 2 needles. When you knit to the middle of a star, you should also automatically reach the middle of a traveling stitch pattern no matter how they look. Each time a star is complete, increase for the sleeve width. Once the sleeve is the desired width, continue working without further increases until the sleeve is the desired length; sleeves often end with a little gusset.

No witchcraft, only skill.

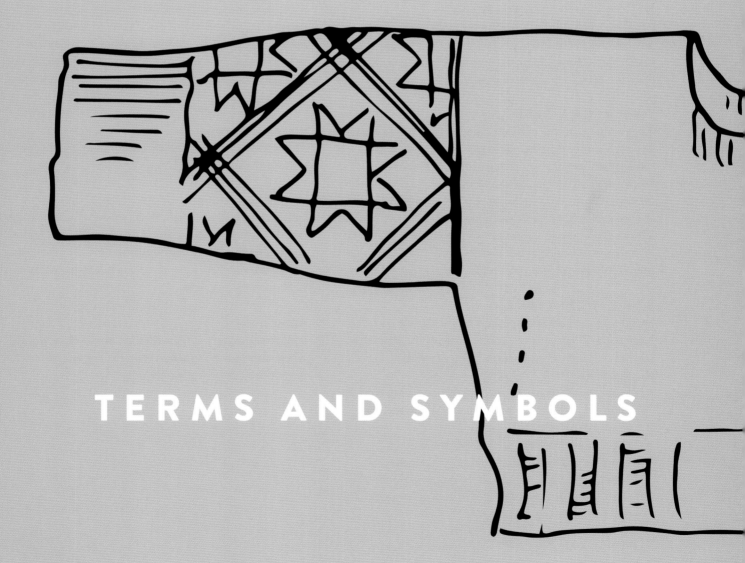

TERMS AND SYMBOLS

KNITTING HELP

YARN

The yarn I used for the sweaters is noted in each pattern. Of course you can substitute other similar yarns/colors. Just be sure that you achieve the correct gauge.

THE CORRECT GAUGE

It cannot be emphasized strongly enough that every new knitting project begins with a gauge swatch. The swatch will let you know whether you need to go up or down in needle size to achieve the gauge given in the pattern.

KNITTED GAUGE SWATCH

Lay the swatch flat and measure off, with a frame or ruler, an area of 4 x 4 in / 10 x 10 cm area. Count the number of stitches and rows in the framed area. Now you can compare your gauge with that given in the pattern.

THE RIGHT SIZE

The sweater patterns in this book are fashioned as closely as possible after the original sweaters. For that reason, there is only one size for each garment. If you want, for example, to knit the Eskilstrup Sweater but wonder if it will be too small, you can knit it on slightly larger needles or choose somewhat heavier yarn and work from the pattern, adjusting the length, or you can simply adjust the charts. Whatever you decide to do, knit, sample, and make your own calculations before you begin. See also page 234.

SET PIECE ASIDE

Sections of the pattern, especially the body, end with "set piece aside." That means: "do not bind off because the stitches will be worked later on." You can follow one of these methods:
- Leave the stitches on a needle (put point protectors at each end of double-pointed needles so the stitches won't fall off).
- Slide the stitches onto a stitch holder.
- Move the stitches to a length of smooth waste yarn long enough to hold all the stitches comfortably (I recommend using cotton yarn, a little heavier than the working yarn).

When you will continue with the held stitches, move them to the working needle as indicated in the pattern.

UNDERSTANDING CHARTS

1 square = 1 stitch and 1 row/round.

Symbols

When knitting back and forth, there can be a difference in your work on the right side and on the wrong side. If you are knitting on a circular, work as for the right side. A blank square means stockinette and a square with an x means reverse stockinette. So, if you are working on the right side, a blank square means a knit stitch and an x indicates a purl stitch. When working on the wrong side, the blank square means a purl stitch and an x is for a knit stitch.

White and yellow squares

These symbols have different meanings depending on the color of the square.

Direction of knitting

Unless otherwise specified, the first row of a chart is on the right side of the piece. Begin at the right side of the chart and work towards the left. If the first row of the chart is for the wrong side, begin at the left side of the chart and work towards the right.

Arrow

Sometimes a chart will have a little arrow to indicate where to begin. If the arrow is on the left side of the chart, begin the work on the wrong side.

YARN INFORMATION

Geilsk yarns, including Cotton and Wool (Bomuld og Uld), are available in North America via:
Nordic Yarn Imports Ltd.
nordicyarnimports.com

A list of retailers carrying Isager Strik yarns, including Tvinni and Tvinni Tweed, is available via:
Knit Isager
knitisager.com

Harrisville yarns, including Shetland, are available directly from:
Harrisville
harrisville.com

BC Garn yarns, including Shetlandsuld / Shetland Wool, are available in North America via:
LoveKnitting.com
loveknitting.com/us

A list of retailers carrying Rowan yarns, including Wool Cotton, is available via:
Rowan
knitrowan.com

Some yarns—Folkedans Danmark yarns, including Tospring and Trekant / Triangle, and Garnudsalg yarns, including Blackhill Linwool and Blackhill CottonWool—may be difficult to find. A variety of additional and substitute yarns are available from:
Webs – America's Yarn Store
75 Service Center Road
Northampton, MA 01060
800-367-9327
yarn.com

LoveKnitting.com
loveknitting.com/us

If you are unable to obtain any of the yarn used in this book, it can be replaced with a yarn of a similar weight and composition. Please note, however, the finished projects may vary slightly from those shown, depending on the yarn used. Try www.yarnsub.com for suggestions.
For more information on selecting or substituting yarn, contact your local yarn shop or an online store; they are familiar with all types of yarns and would be happy to help you. Additionally, the online knitting community at Ravelry.com has forums where you can post questions about specific yarns. Yarns come and go so quickly these days and there are so many beautiful yarns available.

DANISH CLOTHING TERMS

brystdug
: A type of separate sweater front with ribbons for the sleeves, usually knitted for that purpose or perhaps cut out of a night sweater. Worn under the bul (see below) as a faux night sweater (also called a klipfisk).

bul
: A vest-like top of woven fabric or a type of woolen fabric, often with silk ribbons, hooks and eyes, and with or without attached sleeves. In the patterns: The part of a sweater corresponding to the back and front.

hue
: A bonnet-like head covering with a shaped crown and pleated back neck.

huelin
: Stiff piece of cotton with a lace edging attached beneath the *hue* (cap) which sticks out as decoration.

klokke
: A spencer-like, bell-shaped slip either sewn or knitted.

kramvarer
: Goods purchased in town, at markets, or from traveling salesmen.

købetoj
: Fabric, not homemade.

løse ærmer
: Museums have knitted sleeves that either had been sewn onto garment bodies or were meant to have been sewn on.

mamelukker
: On Falster, *mamelukker* are described as decorative sleeves, covering the arms from the wrist and up over the elbow. They are worn under the decorative sleeves (see *pynteærmer* below).

oplod
: A blouse (to wear beneath a night sweater) or the top part of a shift sewn of fine canvas—or a loose bodice (half shift) which could be put on over the actual shift.

pynteærmer
: Wide, loose tube with silk plisse edges as decoration over the night sweater.

spedtröja
: A Swedish night sweater.

strikvarer
: Ready-made knitted items (such as night sweaters, socks, mittens, etc) knitted and intended for sale.

særk
: An under-sweater/dress with or without sleeves, sewn of linen canvas.

KNITTING VOCABULARY

* or ( )	Asterisks in a pattern indicate that the actions between the asterisks are to be repeated. Sometimes, for short repeats, the information is given between parentheses.
///	Three slashes visually represent the slant of stitches or the cast-on row.
1 ridge	2 knit rows worked back and forth (the first row is on the RS) form a ridge on the RS. For a ridge on the RS when working in the round, work 1 purl round on RS.
back of work	The side of the fabric facing away from you.
binde	An old word for "to knit;" see more on page 46.
braid row (*fletgang*)	An old Falster word for a simple row/round of two-end (also called twined) knitting, in which two strands twist around each other and alternate son every stitch; see page 68.
crab stitch	Crab stitch is the single crochet (= British double crochet) stitch worked backwards, from left to right.
damask pattern	A pattern with texture on the surface of the fabric. Usually single-color and worked in knit and purl stitches.
edge stitches	The first and last st(s) of a row.
front of work	The side of the fabric facing toward you.
knitted cast-on (K-CO)	A method for casting on by knitting loops; see page 65.
knytte	An old word meaning "to knit;" see more on page 46.
left needle	The knitting needle held in the left hand.
left side	When the pattern mentions "left side" referring to the garment, it means your left side when you are wearing the sweater.
lænke	An old word meaning "to knit", used on Lolland, Falster, South Zealand, Bogø, and west Møn.
marker(s)	A ring of plastic or simply a small yarn loop, placed on the needle to mark, for example, the spacing of increases.
multiple of	The number of stitches for a pattern repeat; the pattern stitch count is divisible by the multiple. For some of the patterns, a specified number of stitches may be added on one side to insure that the pattern is balanced.

pregle	An old word meaning "to knit;" see more on page 46.
repeat	A section of pattern which repeats horizontally and vertically so that the same pattern covers a larger area.
reverse stockinette (rev St st)	A stitch pattern with purl sts on the RS and knit sts on the WS.
right needle	The knitting needle held in the right hand.
right side	When the pattern mentions "right side" referring to the garment, it means your right side when you are wearing the sweater.
side seam	A narrow vertical panel on each side of the body on old night sweaters, often an extension of the split below; marking where there might have been actual seam.
sl 1 knitwise	Slip 1 st by inserting the needle into the stitch as if to knit, but, instead of knitting it, slide the st over to the right needle.
sleeve seam	A narrow vertical panel, usually only a single stockinette stitch that runs up the sleeve from the center of the underarm where you might otherwise sew a seam.
sprang	A textile technique, with parallel strands twisted around each other to form a netted fabric.
stockinette (St st)	A stitch pattern with knit sts on the RS and purl sts on the WS (= British stocking st).
stolpegang	An old Falster word for ribbing.
traveling stitch	Pattern with a netting of traveling (sometimes crossed) stitches and diamonds.
traveling stitch and star pattern	A pattern with a netting of traveling stitches and diamonds with stars.
two-end knitting	An old knitting technique in which 2 strands twist around each other and alternate. Also called "twined" knitting.
working yarn	The end of the yarn which comes from the yarn ball.

ABBREVIATIONS AND TERMS

BO	bind off (= British cast off)	p	purl
cm	centimeter(s)	pm	place marker
CO	cast on	psso	pass slipped st over
crab stitch	single (British double) crochet worked from left to right	rep	repeat
dpn	double-pointed needles	rnd(s)	round(s)
est	established, that is, continue in pattern	RS	right side
		sl	slip
in	inch(es)	st(s)	stitch(es)
inc	increase	St st	stockinette st (= British stocking st)
k	knit	tbl	through back loop
K-CO	Knitted cast-on, see page 65	tog	together
M1	Make 1 = with needle tip, from front to back, pick up strand between 2 sts and knit into back l oop = left-leaning increase	WS	wrong side
		yd	yard(s)
		yo	yarnover
M1-loop	increase 1 st by making a back wards loop over needle, see page 67	* to *	repeat from * to *

SYMBOLS

☐	On RS: k1.
	On WS, p1.
☒	On WS: p1.
	On WS, k1.
⊙	Yarnover.
⟟	Slip 1 (inserting needle into st as if to knit, slip the stitch to right needle without working it.
⟍	On RS: 1 twisted knit (k1 tbl) = insert needle into back of stitch and knit it.
	On WS: 1 twisted purl = insert needle into back of stitch and purl it.
☑	M1-loop = increase 1 st by forming a backwards loop around the needle; see page 67.
⊔	Kf&b = knit into front and then back of same stitch; see page 76.
◁	1 horizontal stitch; see page 76.
◆	1 horizontal stitch behind 1 twisted knit; see page 76.
△	K2 together = right-leaning decrease on RS.
▲	P2 together
Ɲ	1 stitch of braid; see page 68.
⊟	K-CO (knitted cast-on) = cast on 1 stitch with knitted cast-on method and knit stitch; see page 65.
⊜	BO 1 stitch.
⟋	On RS: K2tog.
⟍	On RS: Sl 1, k1, psso.
⟔	On RS: P2tog.
⟋	On RS: Cross 2 knit sts to the right; see traveling sts, page 72.
	On WS: cross 2 purl sts to the right; see traveling sts, page 74.
⟍	On RS: Cross 2 knit sts to the left; see traveling sts, page 72.
	On WS: cross 2 purl sts to the left; see traveling sts, page 74.
⟋	On RS and WS: Cross 1 knit and 1 purl st to the right; see traveling sts, pages 73 and 75.
⟍	On RS and WS: Cross 1 purl and 1 knit st to the left; see traveling sts, pages 73 and 75.
⟐	On RS: Place first st on a cable needle and hold behind work, place the second st on another cable needle and hold in front of work, knit the 3rd st, k1tbl with st on front cable needle, and knit the st on cable needle behind work.
⟐	On RS: Place first st on a cable needle and hold behind work, place the second st on another cable needle and hold in front of work, knit the 3rd st, k1 (not twisted) with st on front cable needle, and knit the st on cable needle behind work.
⟔	On RS: Place 2 sts on a cable needle and hold in front of work, k2, k2 from cable needle.

BIBLIOGRAPHY

Andersen, Ellen (1960): *Danske bønders klædedragt*. Carit Andersens Forlag.

Andersen, H.C. (1961): Hvad Fatter gjør, det er altid det Rigtige. I: *Eventyr og historier*, bind 11, s. 58-68. Flensteds Forlag.

Andresen, Sine (1846): *Strikkebog til Skole- og Huusbrug*. Boghandler J. Wagners Forlag.

Blicher, St. St. (1839): *Viborg Amt. Bidrag til Kundskab om de danske Provindsers nærværende Tilstand i oekonomisk Henseende*, s. 155-171.

Bonniers store håndarbejdsleksikon (1996), bind 1-20. Bonniers.

Boyhus, Else-Marie (1972): *Lolland-Falster – en historisk billedbog*. Lolland-Falsters historiske Samfund.

Boyhus, Else-Marie (1974): *Landboreformernes bondegård*. Lolland-Falsters Stiftsmuseum.

Clausen, Minna Holm (1969): *Strikkemetoder og strikkede dragtdele – især hos dansk bondestand*. Schweitzers Bogtrykkeri.

Danske folkedragter. 12 farveplancher. Hassing.

Engmark, Ninna (1986): *Falsterske egnsdragter*. Bind 1: Kvindedragt fra Sydfalster. Bind 2: Kvindedragt fra Nordfalster. Bind 3: Mandsdragt. Illustreret af Anne-Grethe Andersen og Ninna Engmark. Museet Falsters Minder.

Gruno, Klavs Espen (2010): *Rasmus Stæhrs dagbog. Indblik i en øbondes liv og dagligdag set gennem hans dagbog fra Farø 1801-1854*. Landbohistorisk Selskab.

Gudmand-Høyer, Kamma (1995): *Folketøj – modetøj 1750-1835. Dragter og dukker – en bog om folkedragter*. Udgivet i anledning af udstilling på Brønshøj Museum.

Gyldendals Sy- og Strikkebog (1940). Gyldendal.

Hansen, Bodil K. (2006): *Familie- og arbejdsliv på landet ca. 1870-1900. En undersøgelse af ægteskabsdannelse, familie-forøgelse og arbejdsliv med særligt henblik på ændringerne i kvindernes arbejde*. Landbohistorisk Selskab.

Hansen, H.P. (1947): *Spind og Bind. Bindehosens – Bindestuens og Hosekræmmerens Saga*. Ejnar Munksgaards Forlag.

Hazelius-Berg, Gunnel (1935): Stickade tröjor från 1600- och 1700-talen. I: *Fataburen. Nordiska Museets och Skansens årsbok*, s. 87-100.

Harlow, Eve (1977): *The Art of Knitting*. Collins.

Højrup, Ole (1978): *Landbokvinden. Rok og kærne – grovbrød og vadmel*. Illustreret af Povl Abrahamsen. Nationalmuseet.

Jensen, Åse Lund og Karen Lind Petersen (1959): *Moderne strik efter danske almuemønstre*. Høst & Søn.

Johnsson, Anna-Margrethe og Museum Lolland-Falster i samarbejde med Danske Folkedanseres Dragtudvalg (2010): *Huelin og susebukser – bondetøj fra Falster 1770-1870*. Katalog fra udstilling på Museum Lolland-Falster.

Junge, Joachim (1798): *Den Nordsiellandske Landalmues Character, Skikke, Meninger og Sprog*. Sebastian Popp, København.

Kragelund, Minna (1978): *Folkedragter. Landboliv i fællesskabets tid*. Illustreret af Beth Beyerholm. Lademann.

Kristensen, Evald Tang (1981): *Gamle kildevæld – portrætter af danske eventyrfortællere og visesangere fra århundredskiftet*. Fotografier af Peter Olsen m.fl. Nyt Nordisk Forlag.

Lorenzen, Erna og Ulla Thyrring (1977): *Folketøj på landet 1830-1880*. Nyt Nordisk Forlag Arnold Busck.

Lærebog i kvindeligt Haandarbejde (1875). Carl Allers Forlag og Tryk.

Moltke, L. (1871-79): Eske Broks Dagbog 1622. I: *Danske Samlinger*, 2. række, bind 6.

Møller, J.S. (1926): *Folkedragter i Nordvestsjælland*. Det Schønbergske Forlag.

Nielsen, Ann Møller (1983): *Pregle, binde og lænke – gammel dansk strikketradition*. Eget Forlag.

Nielsen, Ann Møller (1988): *Alverdens strikning – historie og teknik*. Forlaget Ariadne.

Nielsen, Ann Møller (u.å.): *Historien om ret og vrang – lidt om dansk strikkehistorie*. Eget Forlag.

Pedersen, Inge Lise, under medvirken af Lise Warburg (1987): Strikningens sproghistorie. En historisk og dialektgeografisk undersøgelse af strikning og strikketerminologi i Danmark. I: *Danske folkemål*, 29. bind, s. 99-158. C. A. Reitzels Forlag.

Pedersen, Inge Lise (1988): *Binde, pregle, spita, sticka, sy. Udkast til en kortlægning af nordisk strikketerminologi.* Særtryk. Skrifter frå norsk målførearkiv XL. Indlegg på den tredje nordiske dialektologkonferansen 1988, s. 303-322. Universitetsforlaget, Oslo.

Pedersen, Mikkel Venborg (2009): *I søvnens favn. Om søvn og sovevaner på landet 1600-1850.* Museum Tusculanums Forlag.

Ploug, Mariann (1979): *Strikkede nattrøjer på danske museer.* Danmarks folkelige Broderier.

Ploug, Mariann (1981): *Gamle lollandske strikkemønstre.* Museum Maribo.

Rhode, Peter (1776): *Samlinger til de danske Øers Laalands og Falsters historie.*

Ringgaard, Maj (2010): En silkestrikket spædbarnstrøje fra Lossepladsen. I: *Dragtjournalen,* årg. 4, nr. 6, s. 37-40.

Ringgaard, Maj (2014): Silk Knitted Waistcoats – a 17th-century fashion item. I: eds. T. Engelhardt Mathiassen, M.-L. Nosch, M. Ringgaard, K. Toftegaard and M. Venborg Pedersen, *Fashionable Encounters. Perspectives and Trends in Textile and Dress in the Early Modern Nordic World,* s. 73-105. Oxbow Books, Oxford.

Rutt, Richard (1987): *A History of Hand Knitting.* B.T. Batsford Ltd., London.

Strange, Helene (1934): Husselænkning (Strømpestrikning). I: *Danske Folkemål,* 1934, s. 29-30.

Strange, Helene (1945): *I Mødrenes Spor. Nordfalsterske Kvinders Arbejde gennem halvandet Hundrede Aar.* Red. J.S. Møller. Ejnar Munksgaard, København.

Sundt, Eilert (1867): *Om Husfliden i Norge. Til Arbeidets Ære og Arbeidsomhedens Pris.* J. Chr. Abelsteds Bogtrykkeri.

Thomas, Mary (1972): *Mary Thomas's Knitting Book.* Dover.

Toxværd, Karen, Helene Strange og Elna Mygdal (1926): Den falsterske Dragt, særlig Kvindedragten. I: *Lolland-Falsters historiske Samfund,* Aarbog XIV, s. 1-26.

Warburg, Lise (1980): *Strikkeskeen – et glemt redskab.* Herning Museum.

Warburg, Lise (1989): I silkestrik fra top til tå. Særtryk af *Fru Kirstens børn. To kongebørns begravelser i Roskilde Domkirke.* Nationalmuseet.

Warburg, Lise (1989): Skånske knyttepinde. Särtryck ur *Kulturens årsbok,* s. 63-77.

Wedel, L.M. (1806): *Indenlandske Rejse.* S. Hempel, Odense.

West, Emilie (1889): *Vejledning til methodisk Undervisning i kvindeligt Haandarbejde.* Rom.

Wittgren, Bengt, red. (1986): *Textila tekniker i nordisk tradition.* Rapport från nordiskt symposium om textila tekniker 1986. Uppsala. Luutonen, Marketta, Kalli Klement, Nicolina Jensen, Anne Kjellberg, Gerd Aarsland, Lise Bender-Jørgensen, Lise Warburg, Else Østergård og Marianne Erikson.

www.aksp.dk
www.dragt.dk
www.ods.dk
www.textilnet.dk

ACKNOWLEDGMENTS

WITH THANKS

With thanks to the Museum Lolland-Falster and many other Danish and Swedish museums who have so kindly opened their collections for me.

A very special thanks to Maj Ringgaard, Ph.D., textile conservator at the National Museum of Denmark.

Thank you also to Else Nielsen, Helle Sørensen, and Lis Jensen for knitting the new sweaters.

Thank you to jewelry designer Grete Jørgensen (www.gj.smykker.dk) for the loan of jewelry.

I would also like to thank The Danish Library for their wonderful help. Time and time again, I was amazed at how quickly they brought out rare, often very old, books for me.

Most of all, I want to thank the publisher Ulrik T. Skafte, who dared to jump into the large project of producing this book, and Merete Kjær Petersen for her huge efforts as editor—it has been incomparable.
Thank you for your patience and your many, long linguistic discussions along the way, as the fight bounced back and forth.
Also the graphic designer, Anja Søe, has stretched her bow to the utmost in her zeal for making this book aesthetically pleasing and beautiful. Without you, this book would never have amounted to anything!

Szveba